# U. S. Hood Ornaments and More . . .

## Lynn Huntsburger

PrairieLand Publishing
Sullivan, Illinois

FIRST EDITION

All rights reserved, including the right
of reproduction in whole or in part in any form.

Copyright © 1994 Lynn Huntsburger

Co-Published by:
Lynn Huntsburger
404 W. Roane St., Sullivan, IL 61951
&
PrairieLand Publishing
R.R. #1, Box 93, Sullivan, IL 61951

Manufactured in the United States of America

ISBN: 0-9644110-0-8

---

For additional copies send
$26.95 plus $3.00 P&H to:

Lynn Huntsburger
404 W. Roane St.
Sullivan, IL 61951

# FOREWORD

I will try to give you a short summary of myself, the person that compiled this book.

I have been in the automotive business since World War II. I started O.K. Jobbers in 1946 which sold automotive and industrial supplies and ran an engine rebuilding shop. I sold the business in 1982 and retired. I restored old cars and collected hood ornaments to keep busy.

My wife, Louise, passed away in 1985. I later married my wife's sister, Nancy Wilhelm, following the loss of her husband, Albert, who was killed in an accident. I would like to thank Nancy for putting up with me in working on this book.

Yes, I proudly did all of the things that a businessman does in his community. In addition, I served on the board and was the president of the Automotive Wholesalers of Illinois, located in Springfield, Illinois.

A year or more ago, I received a call from my friend, Bob Corley, a Lion's Club member who had worked on a road rally with me, and he asked me what I was doing. I told him that I was restoring a 1927 Hudson and learning how to run a computer to catalog hood ornaments. All he could say was "good luck" and that I knew just enough about a computer to be dangerous.

I am 80 years old and I can safely say the errors that you may find in this book can be blamed on the computer, as this was the information I received from the various manufacturers when they wrote me in regards to errors on their bills.

I know that you bought this book to look at pictures instead of reading about me, so have fun and enjoy a look back in history!

# ACKNOWLEDGMENTS

I have made the utmost effort to compile the information as accurately as I can, but I am sure that I do have errors and will appreciate your indulgence.

The following people have helped me and I would like to acknowledge them at this time.

I would like to especially recognize Mr. A. F. Cooper from KC, Missouri for without his help I would have been unable to put together this book. I am sure I will omit some that I should recognize but here are some that were a great help in finalizing this book.

| | |
|---|---|
| John Weitlanf | Dayton, Ohio |
| Mike Klrba | Ontario, Canada |
| Norman Phillips | San Diego, California |
| Andy Bembaum | Newton, Massachusetts |
| Steven Ehrlick | Great Bend, Kansas |
| Barb Kap Servis Motors | Cicott, Indiana |
| Gordon Fairbanks | Fort Pierce, Florida |
| Raymond Gansen | Alberta, Canada |
| Bennie Bloodworth | Smyrna, Georgia |
| Bob Fierro | Paterson, New Jersey |
| Benny Korg | Spokane, Washington |
| T. J. Root | Okeene, Oklahoma |
| Hugh Morrison | Nisouri City, Texas |
| Bob Herbst | Thomasville, North Carolina |
| Antique Auto Parts | Spokane, Washington |
| John Crabtree | Newcastle, Wyoming |
| Freemon's | Whitehall, Montana |
| Robert J. Antebi | Mesa, Arizona |
| Bob Boyd | Chetopa, Kansas |

I would like to thank all that made it possible for this book to be published.

Lynn Huntsburger

# 1946 LINCOLN COUPE

This car was will from Garold James York of Strasburg, Illinois to Elvis and Lisa Presley but was never titled to them as both York and Presley passed away about the same time and the Presley estate did not accept it. It was sold at auction and walker construction of Mattoon, Illinois purchased and restored it. I purchased it from Mr. Walker on November 5, 1990 and did some minor repairs to it and it runs and drives great today. The entire information in regards to this York and Presley deal is documented by the Herald & Review article dated June 11, 1978.

# INTRODUCTION

This book is to continue after the radiator cap was replaced by placing the filler under the hood thus opening an area of hood ornaments.

I decided to assemble a book after I purchased the *Motoring Mascots of the World* by William C. Williams. I would highly recommend if you do not have this copy please purchase one as it is very well done and you will have many enjoyable hours looking at it.

There are three manufacturers that have used the emblem on the radiator cap and hood ornament from the early models and have stayed with it to the present manufacturing of their vehicles. Chrysler Dodge division sales and the advertising department picked the ram for its sure-footedness and durability. Various sizes and styles have been used throughout the years but the theme of the ram has been maintained.

The other manufacturer that maintained their mascot throughout their manufacturing is the Mack truck. Their mascot is the bulldog. It was picked because it too represented a tough and rugged dependable vehicle that you could depend on.

Olds division was one of the first to use the jet plane for their vehicles and they still us the jet in a shield for its emblem. There were others that used the jet age on their vehicles.

Nash used the flying lady for some years.

Packard used the swan but changed to different ideas throughout their manufacturing.

There was an area that the aftermarket hood emblem was used to customize their auto, though not a wide scale use, and there are still manufacturers that supply various mascots for sale.

The large hood ornaments were phased out as a safety feature as some of them were made out of lead and were dangerous when there was a wreck, also there was a cost savings for the manufacturer.

Some manufacturers used small emblems on the fenders, but most of them did away with the hood emblems all together.

Finally, some did go back to a small emblem on the hood trying as they did in early years to come up with an emblem to identify their vehicle. Such as Buick with its shield, Cadillac with its wreath and shield, and Olds with its small jet outline. Chrysler corporation used the star. Ford with its name shield, GMC truck used its initials. Others used the painted emblem or name for their identification.

Like all things when there is a cost factor to manufacturing a product many of the frills that were used in the past have to go, I guess this is progress but many of the younger generation will not of had the privilege to have seen what brainstorms that some of the advertising people came up with to attract attention to buy their products.

*U. S. Hood Ornaments and More . . .*

# AUTO BODIES

## *Ford Motor Company*

Talk about recycling Henry Ford did that in the 1900's when he ordered suppliers to ship parts in wood and the sizes were designed so the length could be used in the floor boards and fire wall of his bodies, for he built his own and did not farm them out as the other manufacturers did. Showing the ability to produce and conserve at the same time.

## AUTO BODY MANUFACTURING

### Body by Fisher

They were the major manufacturer for the General Motor car bodies. They used a lot of wood as most car bodies were at that time. It was a specialty field and the car manufacturers were more interested in the mechanical part of the manufacturing. Fisher bodies were well liked in the early days because they were a lot of wood covered with metal which helped deaden the sound of the road and the sound of closing the doors made a solid sound which was pleasing to the buyer. Forming metal of lighter gauge material around wood was easier and cheaper.

U. S. Hood Ornaments and More . . .

# AUTO BODY MANUFACTURING

## Hayes Body Corporation

Hayes bodies were of metal construction and in the early years they did not have the insulating ability at that time even though they were stronger. The road noise and closing of the door was tinny. It took sales people explaining the difference between the two body designs before they were accepted.

U. S. Hood Ornaments and More . . .

# APPERSON BROTHERS CO.

## *Makers of Jack Rabbit Cars*
### *Kokomo, Indiana U.S.A.*

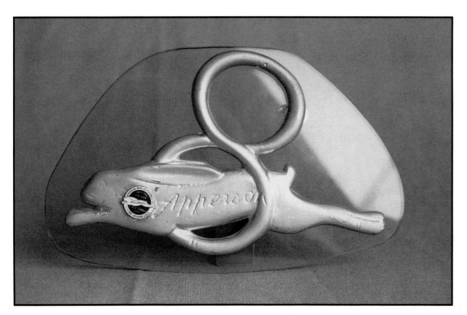

**YEAR:** 1918
**MODEL:** Apperson
**INF:** Jack Rabbit 8; bronze casting

**#0018**

U. S. Hood Ornaments and More . . .

# BROCKWAY

**MODEL:** Brockway
**INF:** Huskie Truck Emblem


**#0050**

*U. S. Hood Ornaments and More . . .*

# BUICK

**YEAR:** 1931-32
**MODEL:** Buick
**INF:** Buick 8
Pat. 82809

**#0031**

**YEAR:** 1934-1935
**MODEL:** Buick
**INF:** T-29726
Series 50-60-90
Goddess

**#0034**

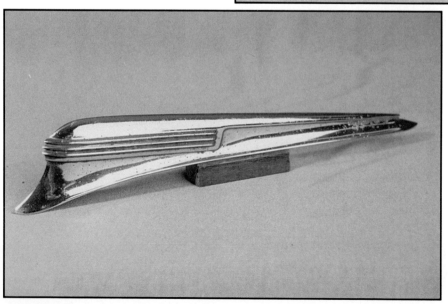

**YEAR:** 1938
**MODEL:** Buick
**INF:** 1304675
9" long

**#0038**

*U. S. Hood Ornaments and More . . .*

# BUICK

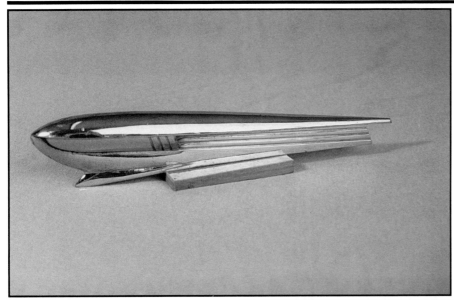

**YEAR:** 1938
**MODEL:** Buick
**INF:** 1298513
1298515
13" long

**#0138**

**YEAR:** 1939
**MODEL:** Buick
**INF:** T-29775
15" long

**#0039**

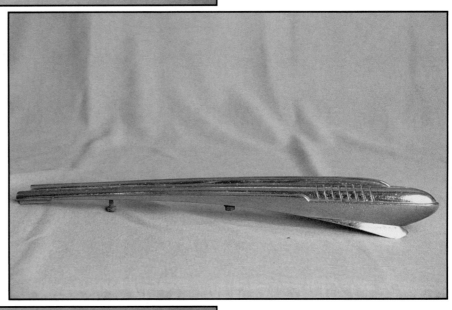

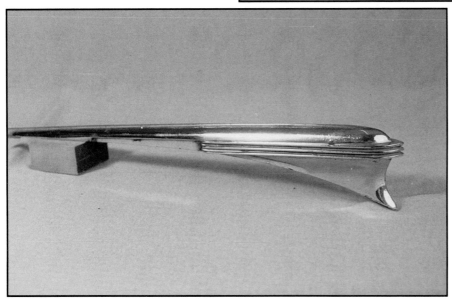

**YEAR:** 1940
**MODEL:** Buick
**INF:** 129794
1345991
14-1/2" long

**#0040**

U. S. Hood Ornaments and More . . .

# BUICK

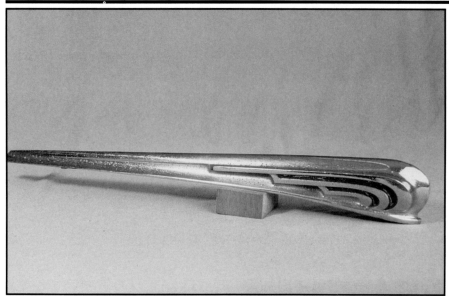

**YEAR:** 1941
**MODEL:** Buick
**INF:** 1320127
18" long

#0041

**YEAR:** 1942
**MODEL:** Buick
**INF:** 373445
Road Master
17" long

#0042

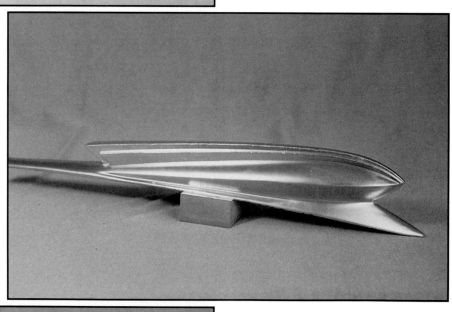

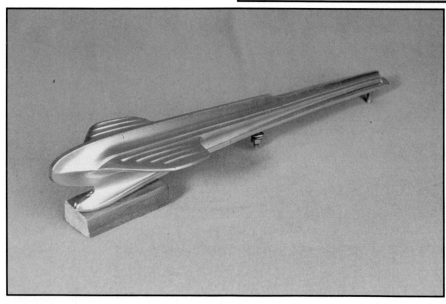

**YEAR:** 1942
**MODEL:** Buick
**INF:** 1323384
18" long

#0142

U. S. Hood Ornaments and More . . .

## BUICK

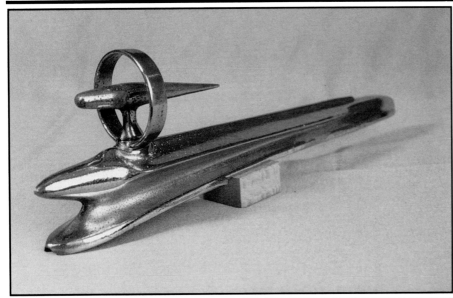

**YEAR:** 1946
**MODEL:** Buick
**INF:** Dynaflow
15" long with bomb sight

**#0146**

**YEAR:** 1946-1949
**MODEL:** Buick
**INF:** 1328355
1393721
16" long base with bomb sight

**#0047**

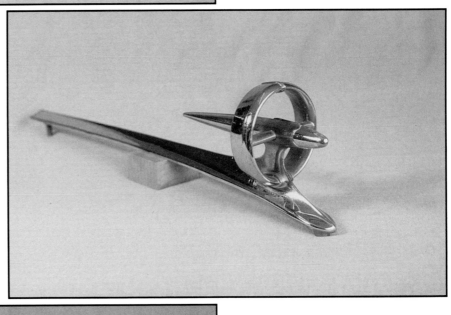

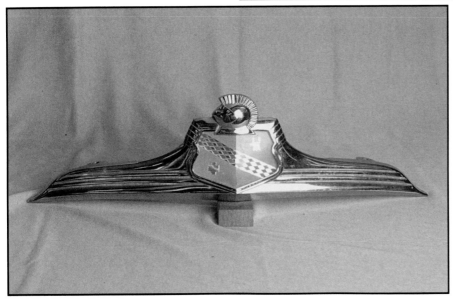

**YEAR:** 1948
**MODEL:** Buick
**INF:** 1336913
Front emblem;
22" wide; 6" tall

**#0148**

U. S. Hood Ornaments and More . . .

# BUICK

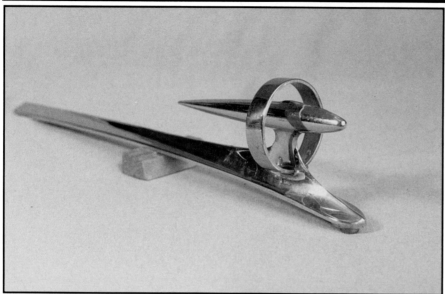

**YEAR:** 1948-1949
**MODEL:** Buick
**INF:** Small Circle with 6-1/2" Spear

**#0048**

**YEAR:** 1949-1950
**MODEL:** Buick
**INF:** 1338878
10" long

**#0050**

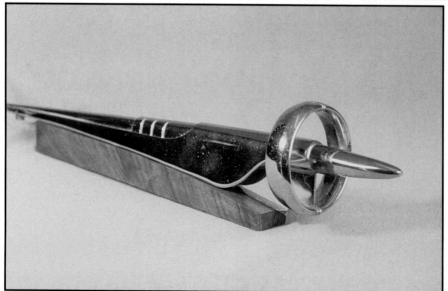

**YEAR:** 1951-1952
**MODEL:** Buick
**INF:** 1342645
Special; 21" long

**#0051**

*U. S. Hood Ornaments and More . . .*

## BUICK

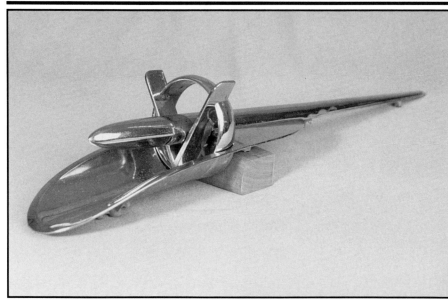

**YEAR:** 1953
**MODEL:** Buick
**INF:** T-1345991
345991
22" long

**#0053**

**YEAR:** 1954
**MODEL:** Buick
**INF:** 1162501
22" long

**#0054**

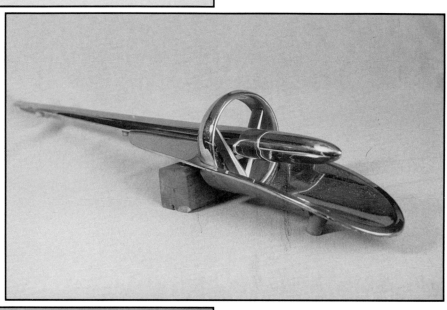

**YEAR:** 1955
**MODEL:** Buick
**INF:** 1166421
9" long

**#0055**

*U. S. Hood Ornaments and More . . .*

# BUICK

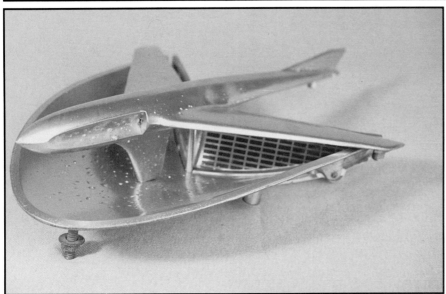

**YEAR:** 1956
**MODEL:** Buick
**INF:** 1170203
Road Master
14" long

#0056

**YEAR:** 1956
**MODEL:** Buick
**INF:** Front Emblem
37" long; 7" circle

#0156

**YEAR:** 1956
**MODEL:** Buick
**INF:** 1162798
Special; 23" long;
4-1/4" red, white
& blue circle

#0356

*U. S. Hood Ornaments and More . . .*

# BUICK

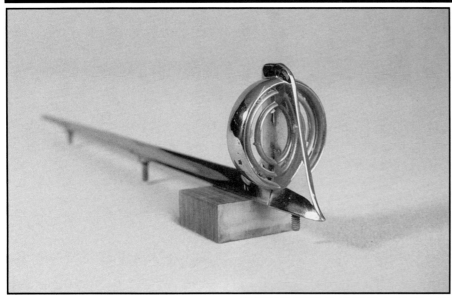

**YEAR:** 1957
**MODEL:** Buick
**INF:** 1174369
Special; 14" long

**#0057**

**YEAR:** 1957
**MODEL:** Buick
**INF:** 1174408-1
Special; red, white & blue; 35-1/2" long; 5-1/4" circle

**#0157**

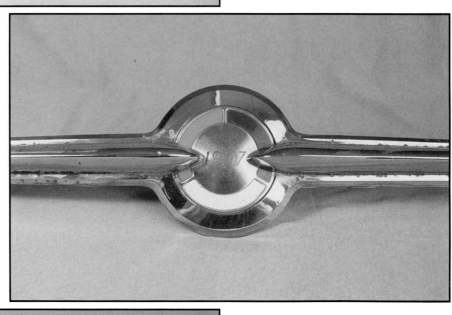

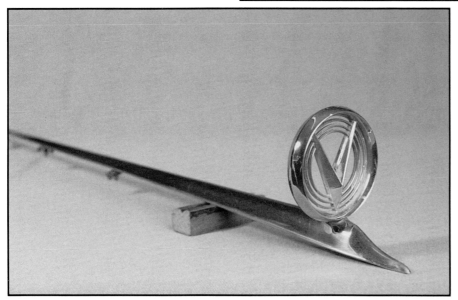

**YEAR:** 1958
**MODEL:** Buick
**INF:** 1182525 LT
24" long

**#0058**

U. S. Hood Ornaments and More . . .

# BUICK

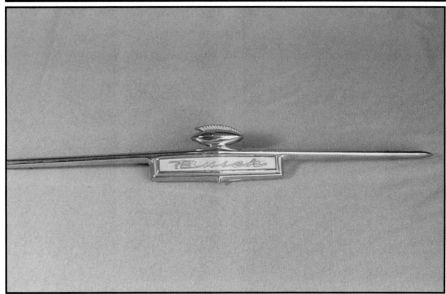

**YEAR:** 1959
**MODEL:** Buick
**INF:** 1186824-C2
Front emblem; 22" wide

#0059

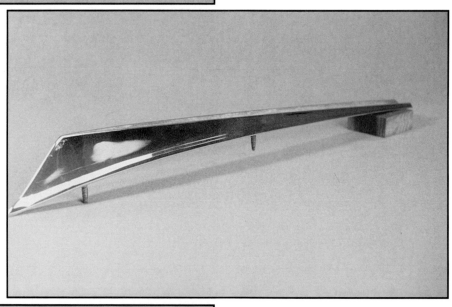

**YEAR:** 1961
**MODEL:** Buick
**INF:** 1199871
18" long

#0061

**YEAR:** 1967
**MODEL:** Buick
**INF:** Regal

#0067

## BUICK

**YEAR:** 1979
**MODEL:** Buick
**INF:** 3 shields; red, white & blue

#0079

**YEAR:** 1981
**MODEL:** Buick
**INF:** 25502269 50274

#0081

*U. S. Hood Ornaments and More . . .*

# BUICK

**YEAR:** 1990
**MODEL:** Buick
**INF:** Buick
3 small shields

#0090

**MODEL:** Buick
**INF:** Buick 8 emblem

#0008

U. S. Hood Ornaments and More . . .

# CADILLAC

**YEAR:** 1930-1932
**MODEL:** Cadillac
**INF:** Goddess; also LaSalle

**#0030**

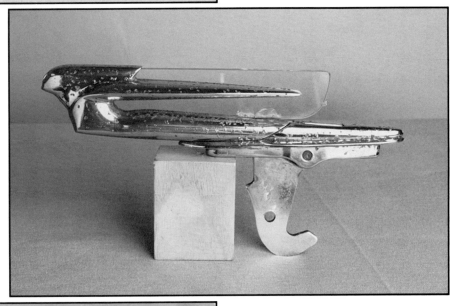

**YEAR:** 1938
**MODEL:** Cadillac
**INF:** Hood release type; also LaSalle

**#0038**

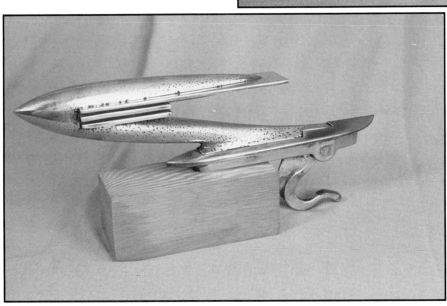

**YEAR:** 1938
**MODEL:** Cadillac
**INF:** LaSalle; latch type with glass wings

**#0138**

*U. S. Hood Ornaments and More . . .*

# CADILLAC

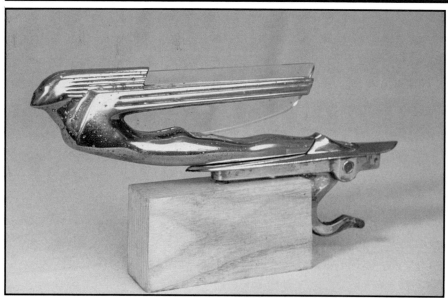

**YEAR:** 1939-1940
**MODEL:** Cadillac
**INF:** Hood release type

**#0039**

**YEAR:** 1941
**MODEL:** Cadillac
**INF:** 3630029
Flowing wings

**#0041**

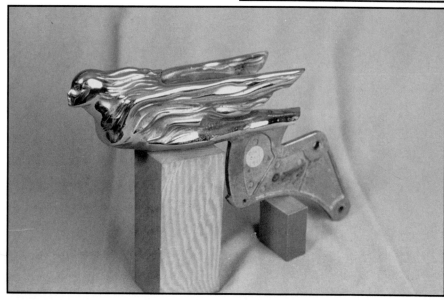

**YEAR:** 1941
**MODEL:** Cadillac
**INF:** 1442135
Hood lock; goddess

**#0141**

U. S. Hood Ornaments and More . . .

# CADILLAC

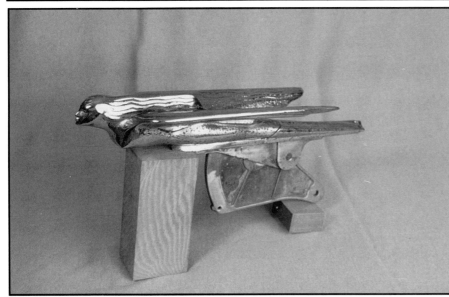

**YEAR:** 1942
**MODEL:** Cadillac
**INF:** 1444490
Hood release;
goddess with flowing hair

#0042

**YEAR:** 1946-1947
**MODEL:** Cadillac
**INF:** 1415009 - Body
1451010 - Tail
Double hood release

#0047

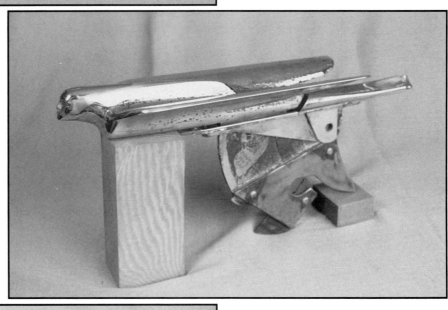

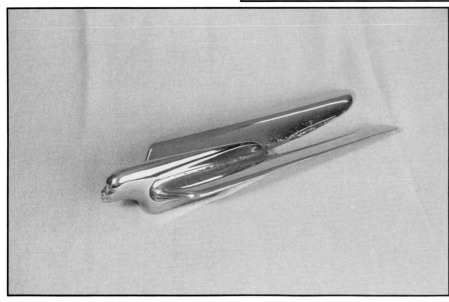

**YEAR:** 1948-1949
**MODEL:** Cadillac
**INF:** 1453909 - Body
Missing tail

#0048

U. S. Hood Ornaments and More . . .

## CADILLAC

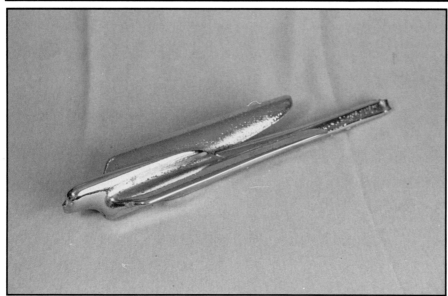

**YEAR:** 1950
**MODEL:** Cadillac
**INF:** 1353909 - Body
1453910 - Tail

#0050

**YEAR:** 1951
**MODEL:** Cadillac
**INF:** 1453909 - Body
1455691 - Tail

#0051

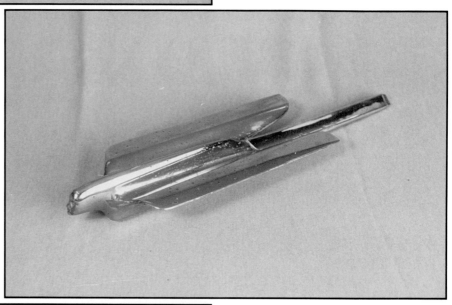

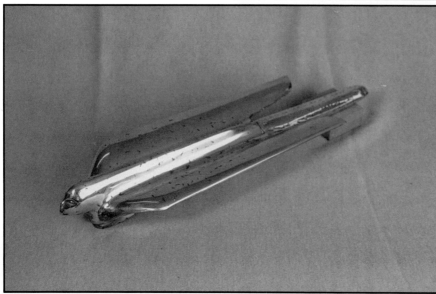

**YEAR:** 1952
**MODEL:** Cadillac
**INF:** 1456354 - Body
1456358 - Tail
Tail extends 4-1/2" past wings

#0052

U. S. Hood Ornaments and More . . .

## CADILLAC

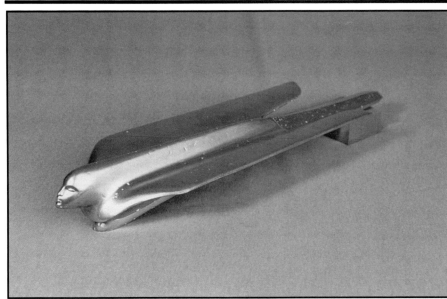

**YEAR:** 1953
**MODEL:** Cadillac
**INF:** 1459707 - Body
1458705 - Tail

#0053

**YEAR:** 1954
**MODEL:** Cadillac
**INF:** 1460581 - Body
0460850 - Tail
Personal car

#0054

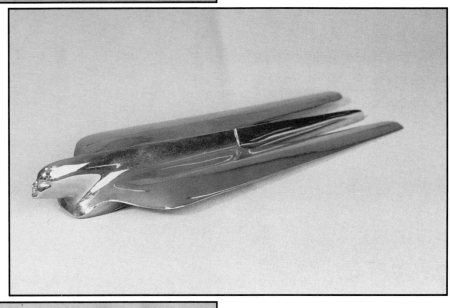

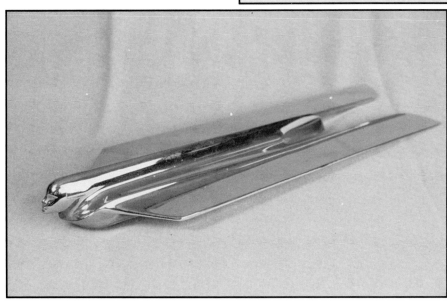

**YEAR:** 1955
**MODEL:** Cadillac
**INF:** 1462532
One piece unit;
wings extend 4" past tail

#0055

*U. S. Hood Ornaments and More . . .*

# CADILLAC

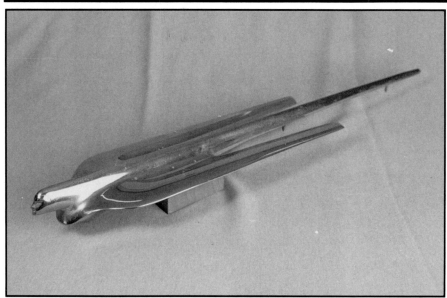

**YEAR:** 1956
**MODEL:** Cadillac
**INF:** 1463388
Long skinny tail

**#0056**

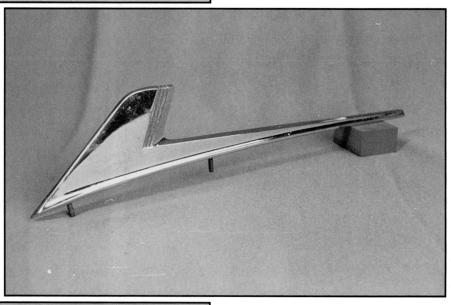

**YEAR:** 1956
**MODEL:** Cadillac
**INF:** 1468802 - RH
1468803 - LH
Fender emblems

**#0156**

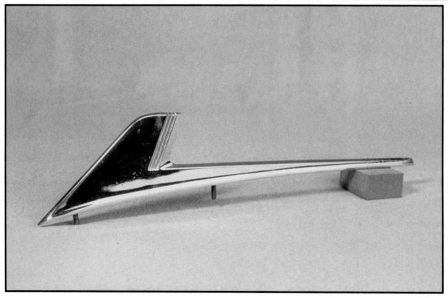

**YEAR:** 1956
**MODEL:** Cadillac
**INF:** 146880 - LH fender

**#0256**

U. S. Hood Ornaments and More . . .

## CADILLAC

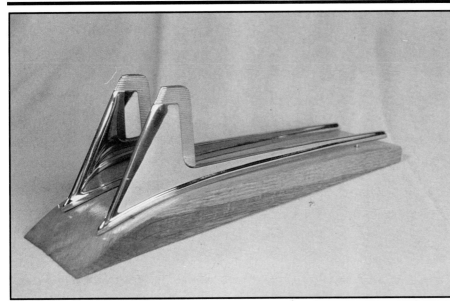

**YEAR:** 1957
**MODEL:** Cadillac
**INF:** 1468005 - LH
1468006 - RH
Hood ornaments

**#0057**

**YEAR:** 1958
**MODEL:** Cadillac
**INF:** Style 57, only larger

**#0058**

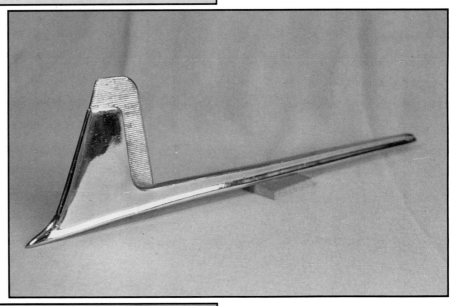

**YEAR:** 1970
**MODEL:** Cadillac
**INF:** 1496978

**#0070**

U. S. Hood Ornaments and More . . .

## CADILLAC

**YEAR:** 1970
**MODEL:** Cadillac
**INF:** Hood emblem

#0170

**YEAR:** 1990
**MODEL:** Cadillac
**INF:** Gold emblem

#0090

**YEAR:** 1990
**MODEL:** Cadillac
**INF:** Standard emblem

#0190

U. S. Hood Ornaments and More . . .

# CHEVROLET

**YEAR:** 1934
**MODEL:** Chevrolet
**INF:** Eagle
Pat. 91300 7-29702

#0034

**YEAR:** 1935
**MODEL:** Chevrolet
**INF:** 94151  7-29735
Eagle Deluxe 1/2 ton

#0035

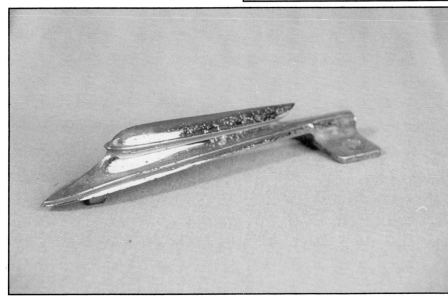

**YEAR:** 1935
**MODEL:** Chevrolet
**INF:** Plain prod.; master

#0235

U. S. Hood Ornaments and More . . .

## CHEVROLET

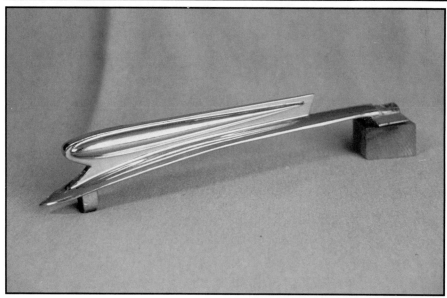

**YEAR:** 1936
**MODEL:** Chevrolet
**INF:** 476338 Prod. no.

#0036

**YEAR:** 1936
**MODEL:** Chevrolet
**INF:** T29765-A  97032
Master Deluxe Eagle;
3-ribbed design

#0136

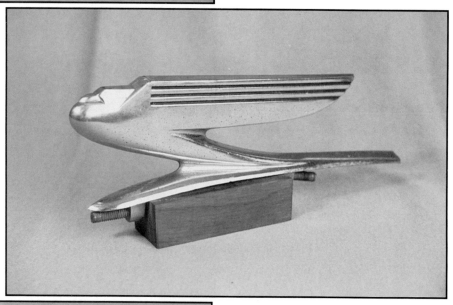

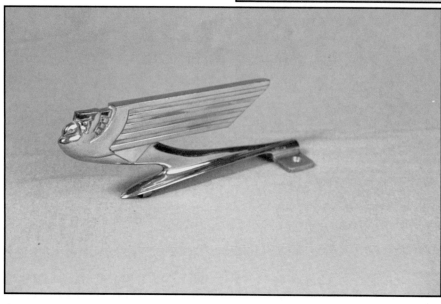

**YEAR:** 1937
**MODEL:** Chevrolet
**INF:** Master Deluxe;
4 ribbed wings;
228 pat. pending

#0037

U. S. Hood Ornaments and More . . .

## CHEVROLET

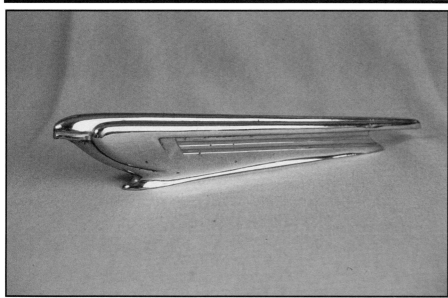

**YEAR:** 1938
**MODEL:** Chevrolet
**INF:** 106474
T29765-A

#0038

**YEAR:** 1939
**MODEL:** Chevrolet
**INF:** T29777

#0039

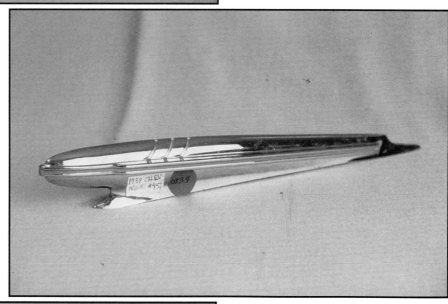

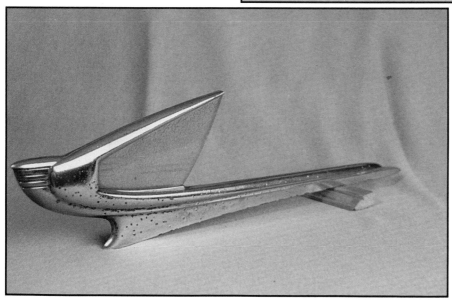

**YEAR:** 1939
**MODEL:** Chevrolet
**INF:** 29784  603476
Wing with glass insert

#0139

U. S. Hood Ornaments and More . . .

# CHEVROLET

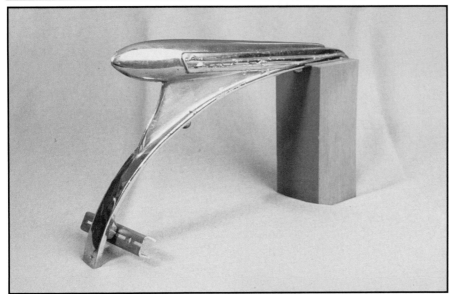

**YEAR:** 1939-1940
**MODEL:** Chevrolet
**INF:** 3650700 4 Coe

#0239

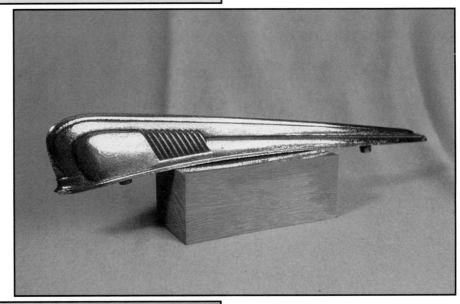

**YEAR:** 1940
**MODEL:** Chevrolet
**INF:** MM 2 986597;
KA, KB, KH standard prod.

#0040

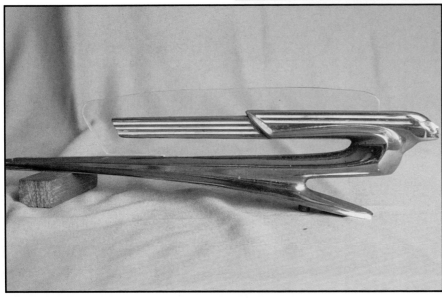

**YEAR:** 1940
**MODEL:** Chevrolet
**INF:** T29804
KA, KH Master Deluxe
604261 Pat. 116467

#0140

## CHEVROLET

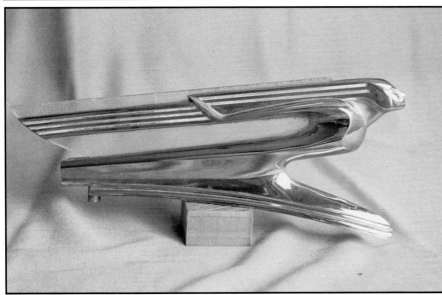

**YEAR:** 1941
**MODEL:** Chevrolet
**INF:** 115467
985710

#0041

**YEAR:** 1941
**MODEL:** Chevrolet
**INF:** 3858321

#0141

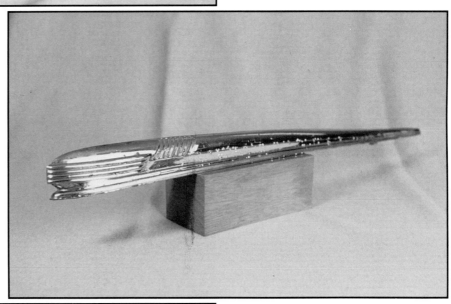

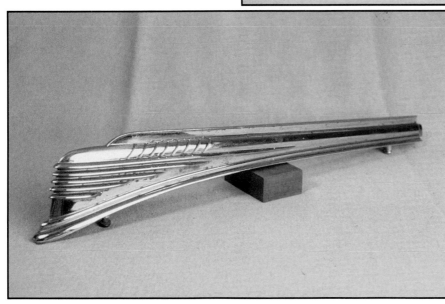

**YEAR:** 1941
**MODEL:** Chevrolet
**INF:** T29810

#0241

U. S. Hood Ornaments and More . . .

## CHEVROLET

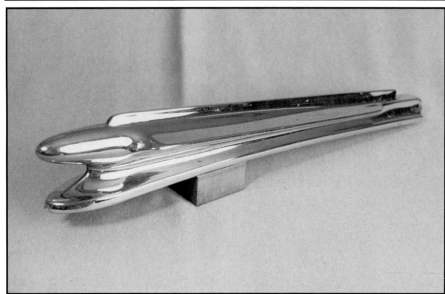

**YEAR:** 1946
**MODEL:** Chevrolet
**INF:** 7106 599858
All chrome

**#0046**

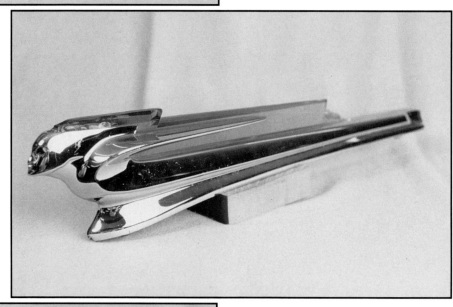

**YEAR:** 1946
**MODEL:** Chevrolet
**INF:** 609581 J7103
Acc. deluxe blue insert

**#0146**

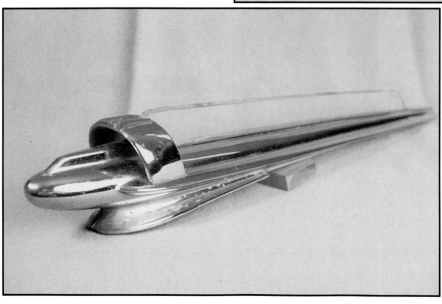

**YEAR:** 1947
**MODEL:** Chevrolet
**INF:** 29804 986107
Deluxe glass insert

**#0047**

U. S. Hood Ornaments and More . . .

## CHEVROLET

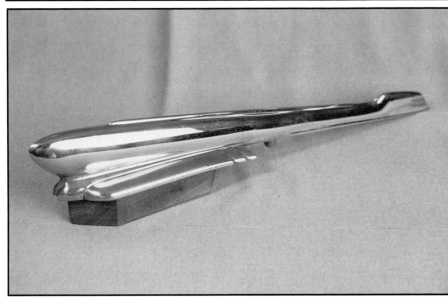

**YEAR:** 1947-1948
**MODEL:** Chevrolet
**INF:** 3684376
Production

**#0147**

**YEAR:** 1948
**MODEL:** Chevrolet
**INF:** 986229
Deluxe glass insert

**#0048**

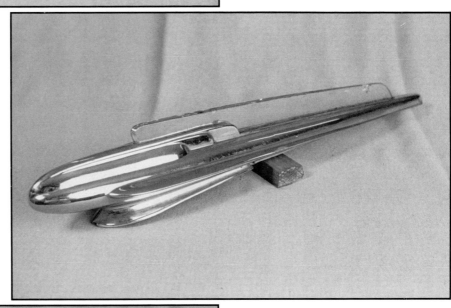

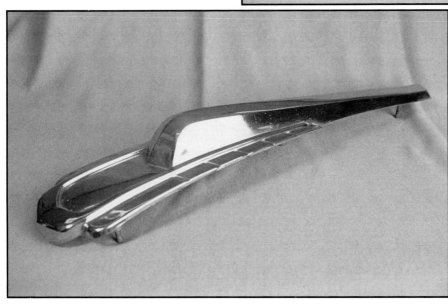

**YEAR:** 1948
**MODEL:** Chevrolet
**INF:** 3688833
Shovel nose

**#0148**

U. S. Hood Ornaments and More . . .

# CHEVROLET

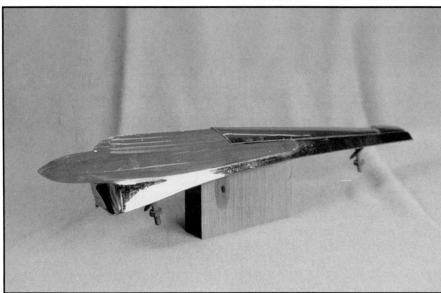

**YEAR:** 1949-1950
**MODEL:** Chevrolet
**INF:** 3687372 986254
Deluxe red insert;
flat design

#0049

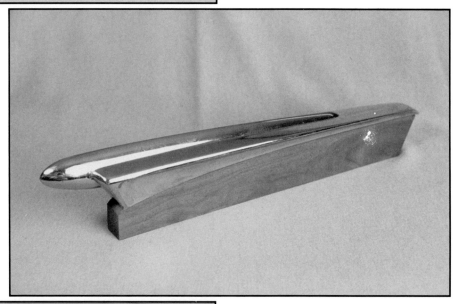

**YEAR:** 1949-1950
**MODEL:** Chevrolet
**INF:** 3686253

#0149

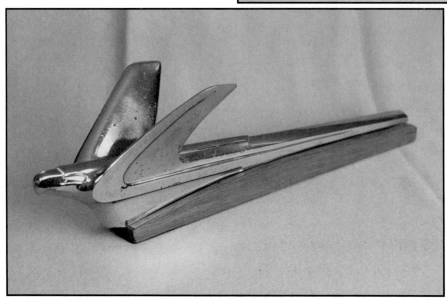

**YEAR:** 1950
**MODEL:** Chevrolet
**INF:** 3694265 986410
High winged eagle

#0050

U. S. Hood Ornaments and More . . .

# CHEVROLET

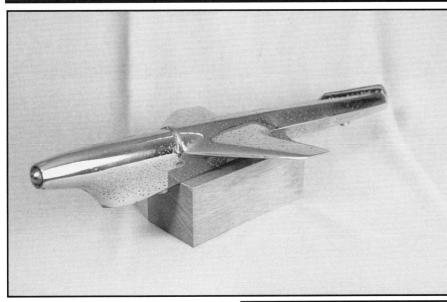

**YEAR:** 1951
**MODEL:** Chevrolet
**INF:** G.M.C. 1 3695337
Standard production

#0051

**YEAR:** 1951
**MODEL:** Chevrolet
**INF:** 3695865
Gazelle

#0151

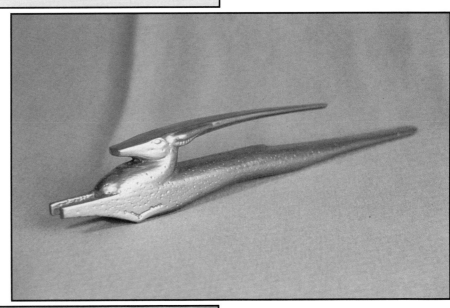

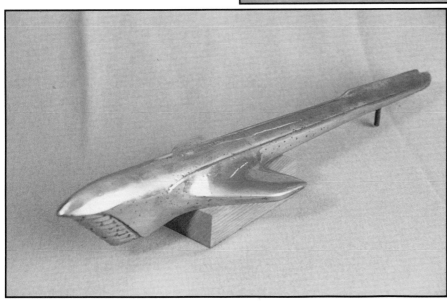

**YEAR:** 1952
**MODEL:** Chevrolet
**INF:** 3699491

#0052

U. S. Hood Ornaments and More . . .

## CHEVROLET

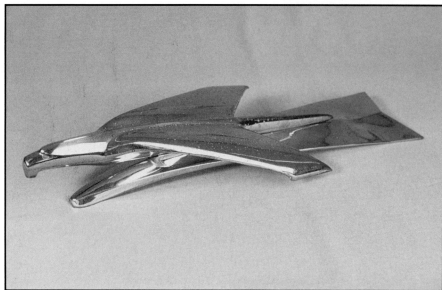

**YEAR:** 1953-1954
**MODEL:** Chevrolet
**INF:** 3701559 3701861
Standard production

#0053

**YEAR:** 1953-1954
**MODEL:** Chevrolet
**INF:** 3701859 3701860
Turned down wings

#0153

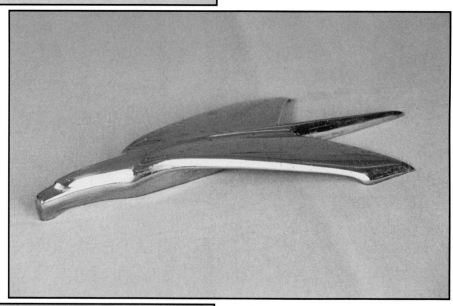

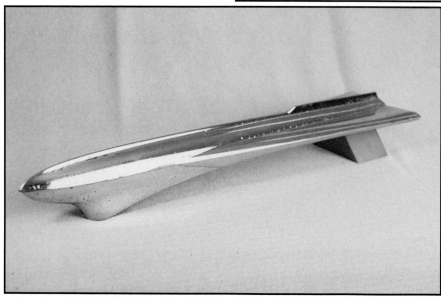

**YEAR:** 1953-1954
**MODEL:** Chevrolet
**INF:** 3701529
Production no.

#0253

## CHEVROLET

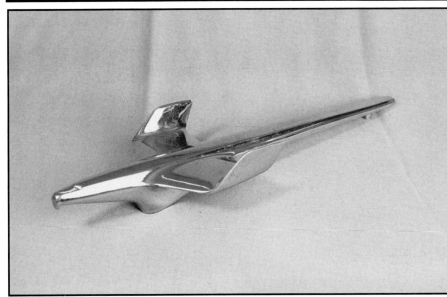

**YEAR:** 1954
**MODEL:** Chevrolet
**INF:** P 3705036-C-1
Wings turned up

#0054

**YEAR:** 1954
**MODEL:** Chevrolet
**INF:** 1750
15" long; 1-7/8" wide;
hood curve

#0454

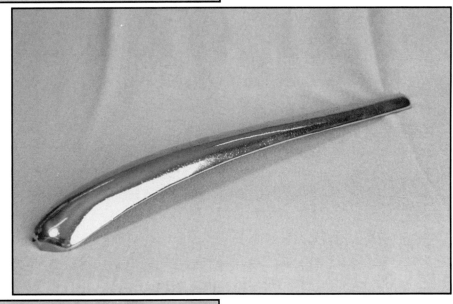

**YEAR:** 1955
**MODEL:** Chevrolet
**INF:** 3709865
Wing fins

#0055

U. S. Hood Ornaments and More . . .

# CHEVROLET

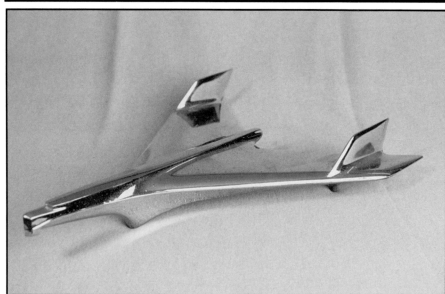

**YEAR:** 1956
**MODEL:** Chevrolet
**INF:** 3731752 3720959
Bel Air

**#0056**

**YEAR:** 1957
**MODEL:** Chevrolet
**INF:** 3738978
RH hood emblem

**#0057**

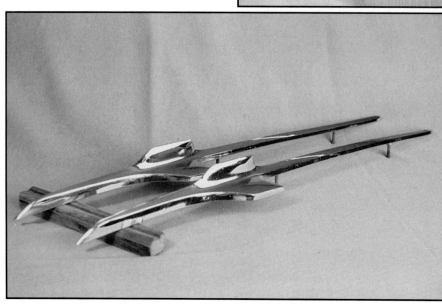

**YEAR:** 1957
**MODEL:** Chevrolet
**INF:** 3723962
(2) fender

**#0157**

U. S. Hood Ornaments and More . . .

## CHEVROLET

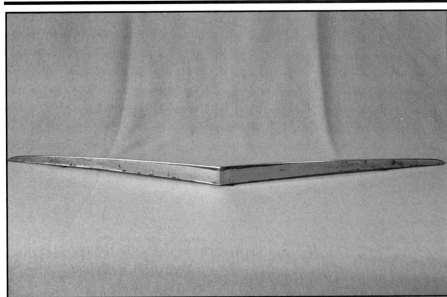

**YEAR:** 1957
**MODEL:** Chevrolet
**INF:** P-3733685
Hood V

**#0257**

**YEAR:** 1958
**MODEL:** Chevrolet
**INF:** 2 P 3750254
Fender; 14" long

**#0058**

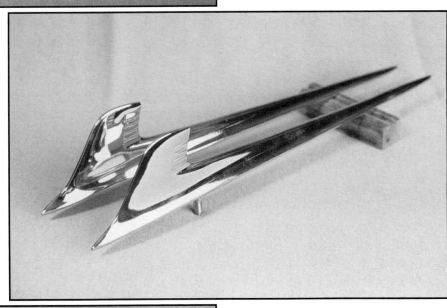

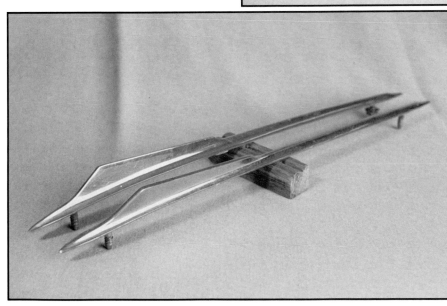

**YEAR:** 1959
**MODEL:** Chevrolet
**INF:** 3756817
3756818
Fender

**#0059**

U. S. Hood Ornaments and More . . .

## CHEVROLET

**YEAR:** 1962
**MODEL:** Chevrolet
**INF:** 3813428 RH
3813427 LH
Fender

#0062

**YEAR:** 1966
**MODEL:** Chevrolet
**INF:** Corvette Sting Ray

#0066

**YEAR:** 1966
**MODEL:** Chevrolet
**INF:** Flags for Corvette Sting Ray

#0166

*U. S. Hood Ornaments and More . . .*

# CHEVROLET

**YEAR:** 1977
**MODEL:** Chevrolet
**INF:** Spring-loaded emblem

**#0077**

**MODEL:** Chevrolet
**INF:** P395619 3942770 Trademark emblem

**#0401**

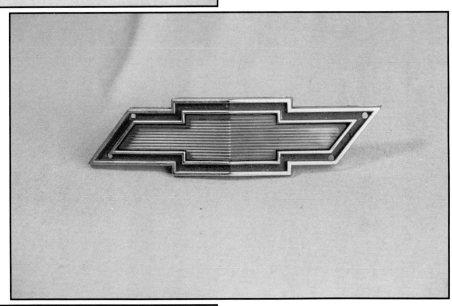

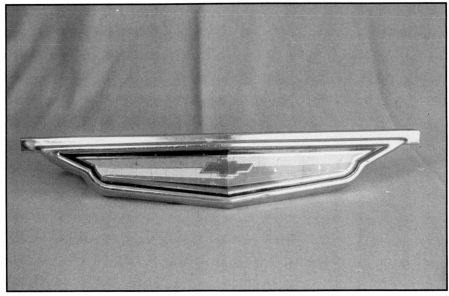

**MODEL:** Chevrolet
**INF:** Front end accessory

**#0402**

U. S. Hood Ornaments and More . . .

# CHEVROLET

**MODEL:** Chevrolet
**INF:** 349690 DS11
Scottsdale 10

**#0403**

**MODEL:** Chevrolet
**INF:** Pat. 3994683
Cheyenne 10

**#0404**

**MODEL:** Chevrolet
**INF:** 3991173
Biscayne

**#0405**

U. S. Hood Ornaments and More . . .

## CHEVROLET

**MODEL:** Chevrolet
**INF:** 337693
Impala

**#0406**

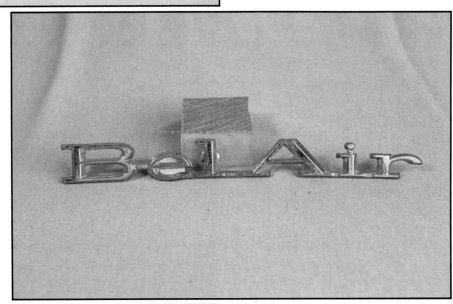

**MODEL:** Chevrolet
**INF:** 7657-786
Bel Air

**#0407**

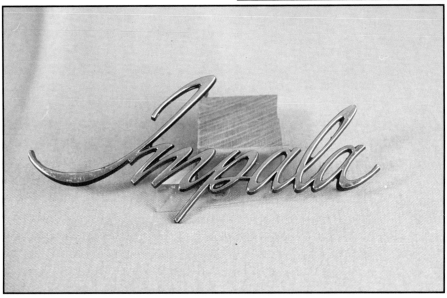

**MODEL:** Chevrolet
**INF:** 3941257
Impala

**#0408**

U. S. Hood Ornaments and More . . .

# CHEVROLET

**MODEL:** Chevrolet
**INF:** 7752901
Camaro

#0409

**MODEL:** Chevrolet
**INF:** Impala script

#0410

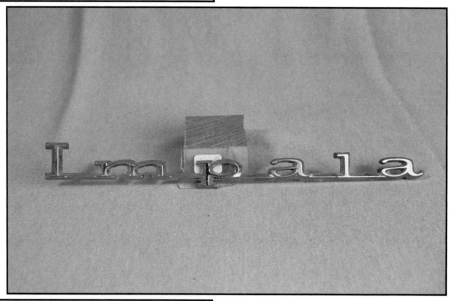

**MODEL:** Chevrolet
**INF:** Caprice script

#0411

U. S. Hood Ornaments and More . . .

## CHEVROLET

**MODEL:** Chevrolet
**INF:** 339241
Chevrolet

#0412

**MODEL:** Chevrolet
**INF:** 325272 3303
Monte Carlo

#0413

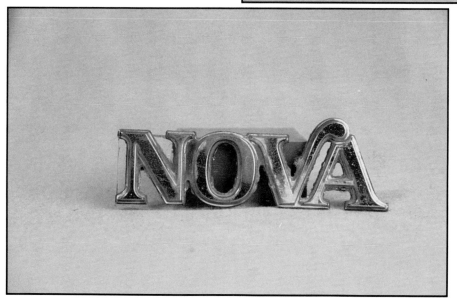

**MODEL:** Chevrolet
**INF:** 1700878
Nova script

#0414

U. S. Hood Ornaments and More . . .

# CHEVROLET

**MODEL:** Chevrolet
**INF:** 3975410
454 number

#0415

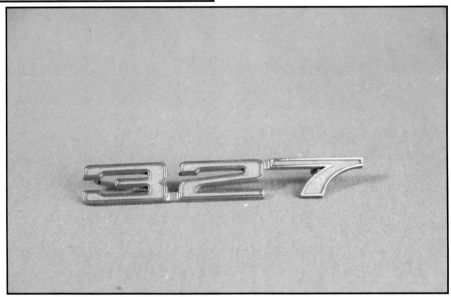

**MODEL:** Chevrolet
**INF:** 3927481
327 number

#0416

**MODEL:** Chevrolet
**INF:** 3827300
SS Impala

#0417

U. S. Hood Ornaments and More . . .

# CHEVROLET

**MODEL:** Chevrolet
**INF:** 3942778
'By Chevrolet'

**#0418**

**MODEL:** Chevrolet
**INF:** Impala
7650313
Side emblem

**#0419**

**MODEL:** Chevrolet
**INF:** Name plate

**#0420**

*United States Hood Ornaments and More . . .*

# CHEVROLET

**MODEL:** Chevrolet
**INF:** Classic Caprice

#0421

**MODEL:** Chevrolet
**INF:** Classic script

#0422

**MODEL:** Chevrolet
**INF:** Camaro name plate

#0423

U. S. Hood Ornaments and More . . .

## CHEVROLET

**MODEL:** Chevrolet
**INF:** 3962949
350 emblem

#0424

**MODEL:** Chevrolet
**INF:** 3972933
350 emblem

#0425

**MODEL:** Chevrolet
**INF:** Vega by Chevrolet
9614435

#0426

*U. S. Hood Ornaments and More . . .*

## CHEVROLET

**MODEL:** Chevrolet
**INF:** 3975418
SS 454

#0427

**MODEL:** Chevrolet
**INF:** #454 Side emblem

#0428

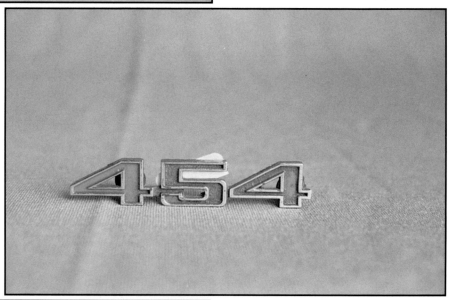

**MODEL:** Chevrolet
**INF:** 3994686
Super

#0429

*U. S. Hood Ornaments and More . . .*

# CHEVROLET

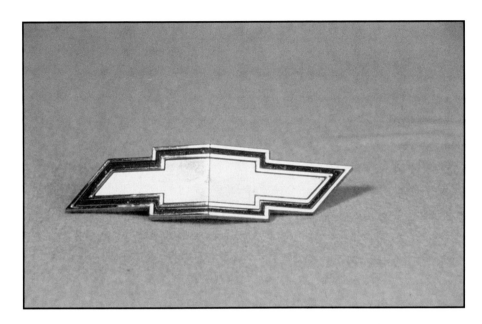

**MODEL:** Chevrolet
**INF:** 6262301
32913

#0430

**MODEL:** Chevrolet
**INF:** G.M-C-4
Nose emblem

#0431

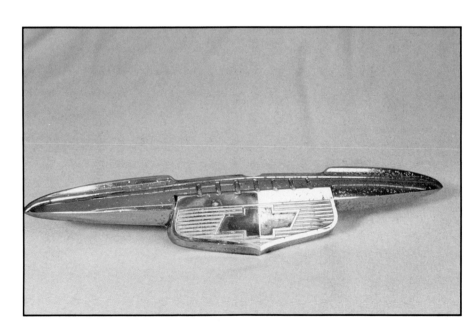

## CHRYSLER

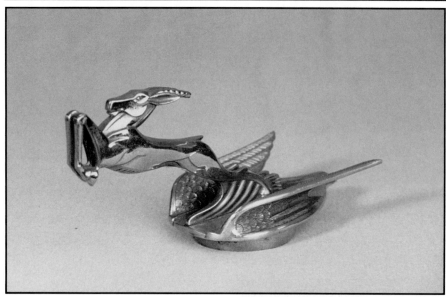

**YEAR:** 1931-1932
**MODEL:** Chrysler
**INF:** Winged cap with gazelle

#0032

**YEAR:** 1935
**MODEL:** Chrysler
**INF:** 634177
Wings

#0035

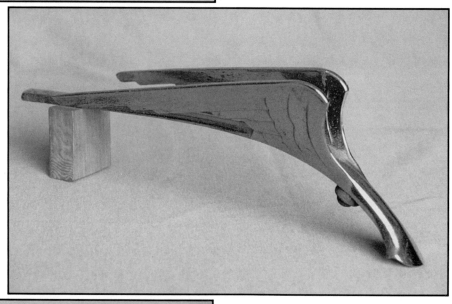

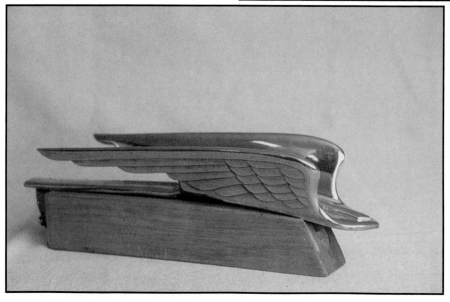

**YEAR:** 1936
**MODEL:** Chrysler
**INF:** 654718
Wings; C 7-8-9

#0036

## CHRYSLER

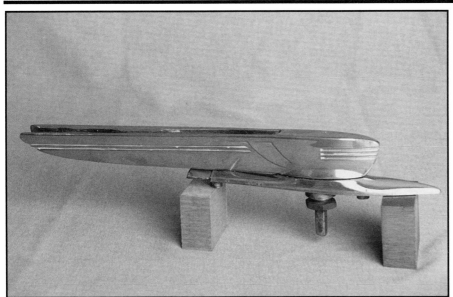

**YEAR:** 1937
**MODEL:** Chrysler
**INF:** 746011 746012;
C 14-15-16

**#0037**

**YEAR:** 1939
**MODEL:** Chrysler
**INF:** 794404 3806
Imperial; C 22-23-24

**#0039**

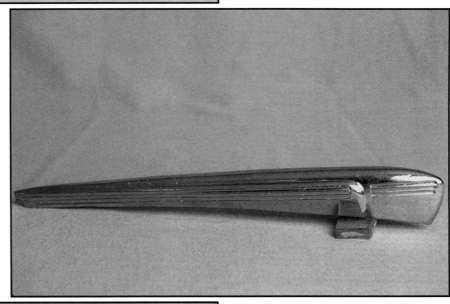

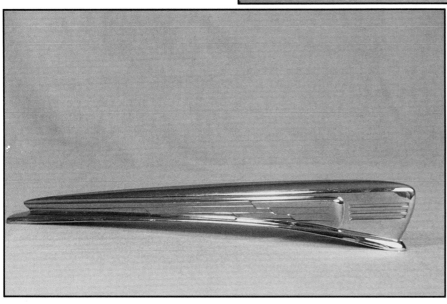

**YEAR:** 1940
**MODEL:** Chrysler
**INF:** 876143
C25-C26-C27

**#0040**

U. S. Hood Ornaments and More . . .

## CHRYSLER

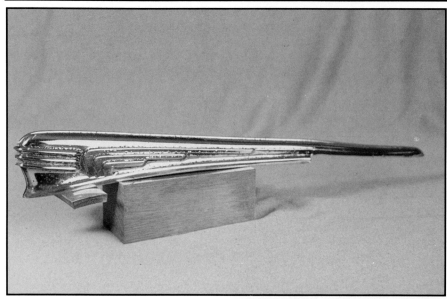

**YEAR:** 1941
**MODEL:** Chrysler
**INF:** 90844 4746
23" long

**#0041**

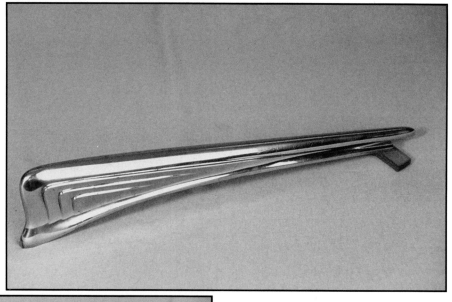

**YEAR:** 1942
**MODEL:** Chrysler
**INF:** 974344 5430 A
16-3/4"; lead

**#0042**

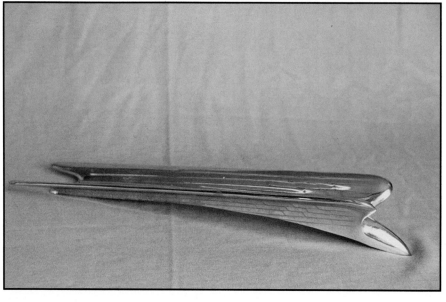

**YEAR:** 1946-1948
**MODEL:** Chrysler
**INF:** 1152452 A11

**#0046**

U. S. Hood Ornaments and More . . .

## CHRYSLER

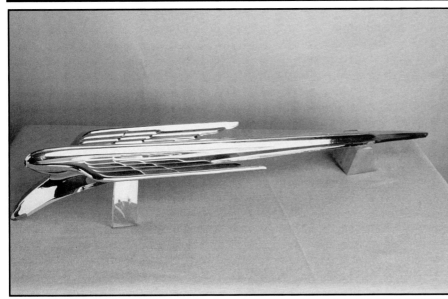

**YEAR:** 1949
**MODEL:** Chrysler
**INF:** 1299366
6 & 8; Imperial

**#0049**

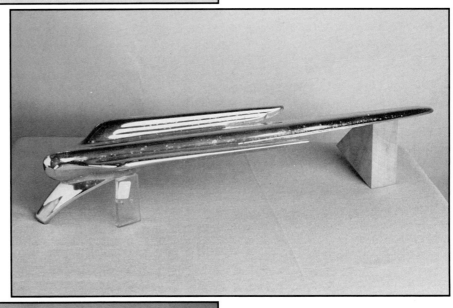

**YEAR:** 1950
**MODEL:** Chrysler
**INF:** 1335540
6 & 8

**#0050**

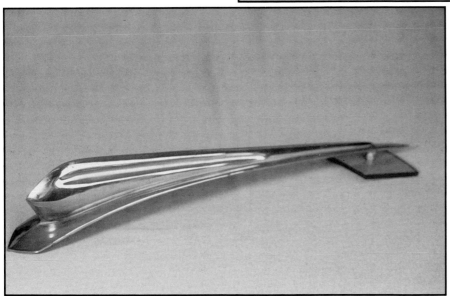

**YEAR:** 1951
**MODEL:** Chrysler
**INF:** 1434605
Plain

**#0051**

U. S. Hood Ornaments and More . . .

# CHRYSLER

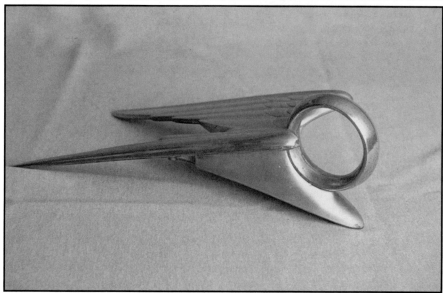

**YEAR:** 1951-1952
**MODEL:** Chrysler
**INF:** 1373208
Imperial; ring with wings

#0052

**YEAR:** 1951-1952
**MODEL:** Chrysler
**INF:** 1373208
New Yorker; ring with wings

#0152

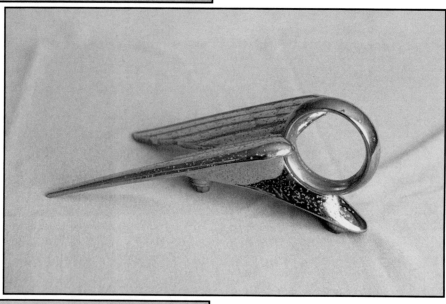

**YEAR:** 1953-1954
**MODEL:** Chrysler
**INF:** 1456742
Imperial; C58-9-64-6

#0053

## CHRYSLER

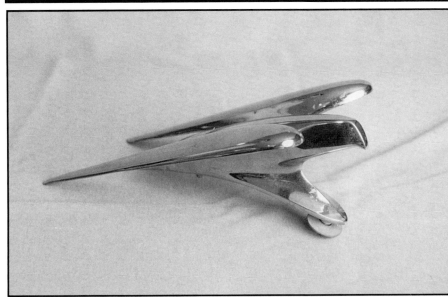

**YEAR:** 1954
**MODEL:** Chrysler
**INF:** 1456679
C56-60-62-63

#0054

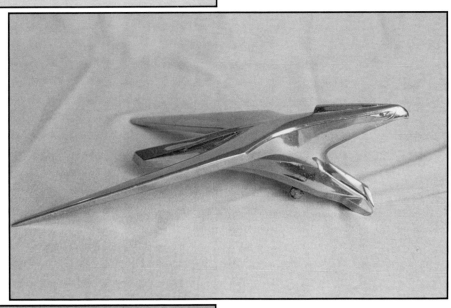

**YEAR:** 1955
**MODEL:** Chrysler
**INF:** 1599858
Eagle with wings

#0055

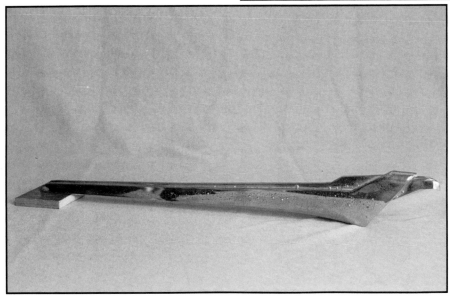

**YEAR:** 1958
**MODEL:** Chrysler
**INF:** 1754960

#0058

U. S. Hood Ornaments and More . . .

## CHRYSLER

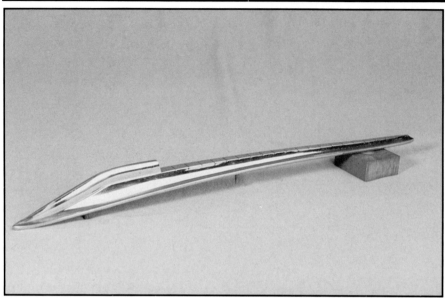

YEAR: 1959
MODEL: Chrysler
INF: 1832982
Fender ornament

#0059

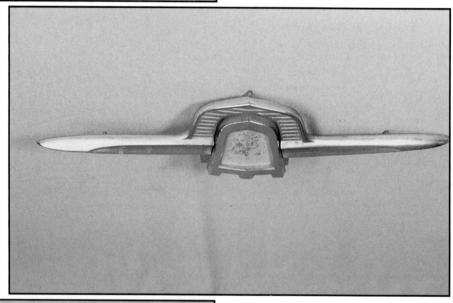

YEAR: 1959
MODEL: Chrysler
INF: 1502711
1902749

#0159

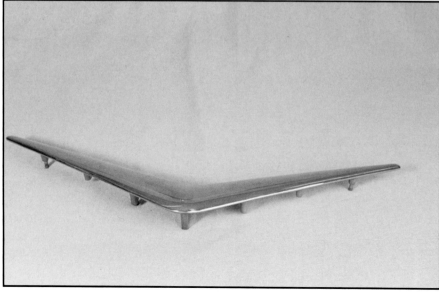

YEAR: 1959
MODEL: Chrysler
INF: Royal Australia

#0259

## CHRYSLER

**YEAR:** 1975
**MODEL:** Chrysler
**INF:** Cordova hood and side emblems

#0075

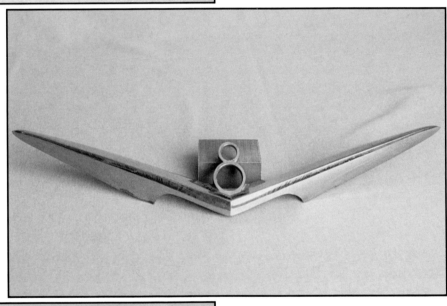

**MODEL:** Chrysler
**INF:** 1593964
V with 8 in center

#0101

**MODEL:** Chrysler
**INF:** 3444194 18700
Script

#0102

*U. S. Hood Ornaments and More . . .*

## CHRYSLER

**MODEL:** Chrysler
**INF:** 3613273 58395
A Special Edition

#0103

**MODEL:** Chrysler
**INF:** Emblem

#0104

U. S. Hood Ornaments and More . . .

# CROSLEY

**YEAR:** 1946-1947
**MODEL:** Crosley
**INF:** Nose has cross T with white jewel

#0047

**YEAR:** 1951-1952
**MODEL:** Crosley
**INF:** Super Deluxe

#0051

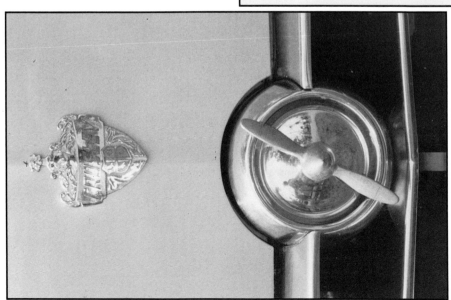

**YEAR:** 1951-1952
**MODEL:** Crosley
**INF:** Bird, emblem and propeller

#0052

U. S. Hood Ornaments and More . . .

# DESOTO

**YEAR:** 1933
**MODEL:** DeSoto
**INF:** 605579
Goddess cap

#0033

**YEAR:** 1934
**MODEL:** DeSoto
**INF:** 471034
Airflow; courtesy of Hubert McCoy

#0034

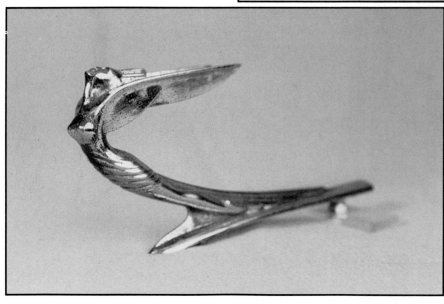

**YEAR:** 1934-1935
**MODEL:** DeSoto
**INF:** 639660

#0134

## DESOTO

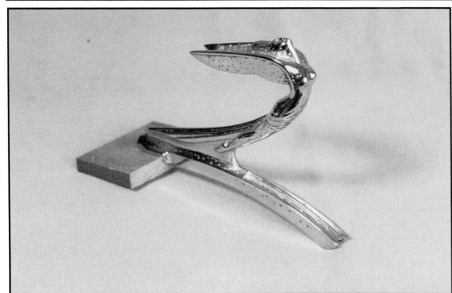

**YEAR:** 1935-1936
**MODEL:** DeSoto
**INF:** 657961
Airflow

**#0035**

**YEAR:** 1935-1936
**MODEL:** DeSoto
**INF:** 654396 654937
Airstream SF SG

**#0135**

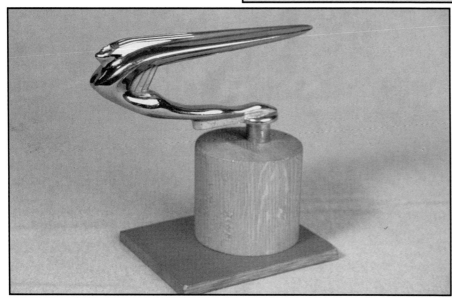

**YEAR:** 1937
**MODEL:** DeSoto
**INF:** Airstream 763708
To open hood

**#0037**

U. S. Hood Ornaments and More . . .

## DESOTO

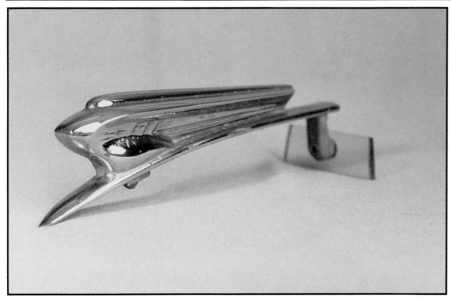

**YEAR:** 1938
**MODEL:** DeSoto
**INF:** 758963

#0038

**YEAR:** 1939
**MODEL:** DeSoto
**INF:** 794089

#0039

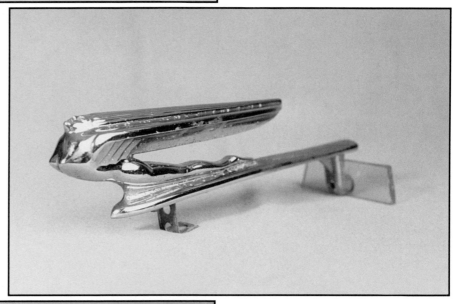

**YEAR:** 1939-1940
**MODEL:** DeSoto
**INF:** 768963
Glass insert

#0040

## DESOTO

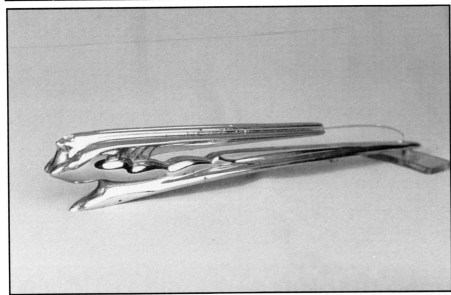

YEAR: 1941
MODEL: DeSoto
INF: 901946 4834-A

#0041

YEAR: 1942
MODEL: DeSoto
INF: 976217
Club Coupe; optional; clear; courtesy of Hubert McCoy

#0042

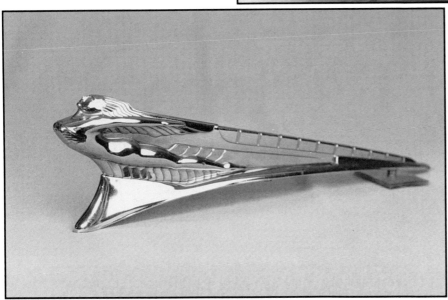

YEAR: 1942-1948
MODEL: DeSoto
INF: 976218
Goddess; 17"

#0046

U. S. Hood Ornaments and More . . .

## DESOTO

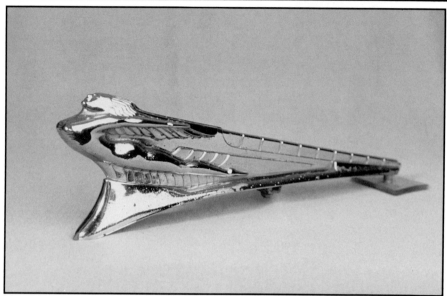

**YEAR:** 1946-1947
**MODEL:** DeSoto
**INF:** 970218 5424
Goddess; 15" long

**#0146**

**YEAR:** 1949
**MODEL:** DeSoto
**INF:** 1298378
23-1/2" long

**#0049**

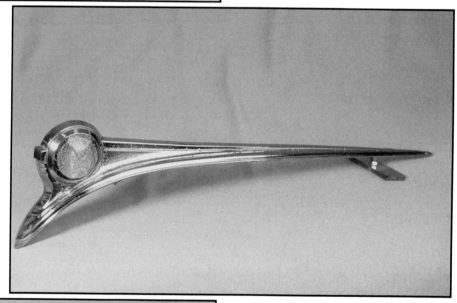

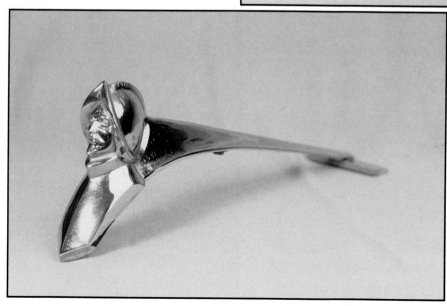

**YEAR:** 1949-1950
**MODEL:** DeSoto
**INF:** 11335605 17559
20-1/2" long

**#0050**

*U. S. Hood Ornaments and More . . .*

# DESOTO

**YEAR:** 1949-1950
**MODEL:** DeSoto
**INF:** 1385606 17569
20-1/2" long; Deluxe

**#0150**

**YEAR:** 1951
**MODEL:** DeSoto
**INF:** 1347334 CB 18496
18-1/4" long with plastic face

**#0051**

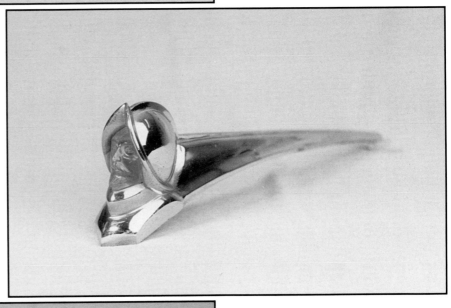

**YEAR:** 1952
**MODEL:** DeSoto
**INF:** 1456510

**#0052**

*U. S. Hood Ornaments and More . . .*

## DESOTO

**YEAR:** 1953
**MODEL:** DeSoto
**INF:** 1456937
12" long; 15" wide

#0053

**YEAR:** 1955
**MODEL:** DeSoto
**INF:** 1599799
10383

#0155

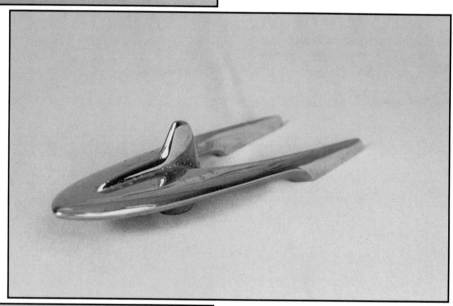

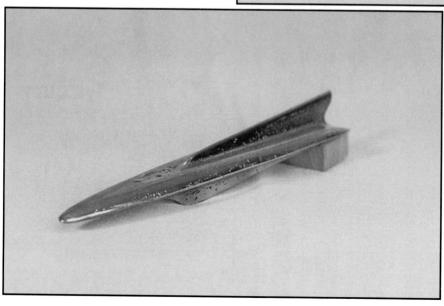

**YEAR:** 1957-1958
**MODEL:** DeSoto
**INF:** Fireflite
1624990

#0057

U. S. Hood Ornaments and More . . .

## DODGE

**YEAR:** 1932-1934
**MODEL:** Dodge
**INF:** Pat. 86370
Ram on cap

**#0032**

**YEAR:** 1935
**MODEL:** Dodge
**INF:** 634173 2826
Ram on rocky strip

**#0035**

**YEAR:** 1936
**MODEL:** Dodge
**INF:** 651992
Ram on plain strip

**#0036**

*U. S. Hood Ornaments and More . . .*

# DODGE

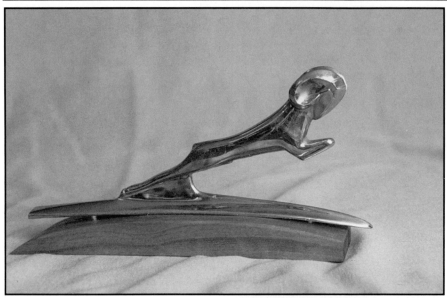

**YEAR:** 1937-1938
**MODEL:** Dodge
**INF:** 746106
Ram

**#0038**

**YEAR:** 1938
**MODEL:** Dodge
**INF:** 768944
Ram on strip

**#0138**

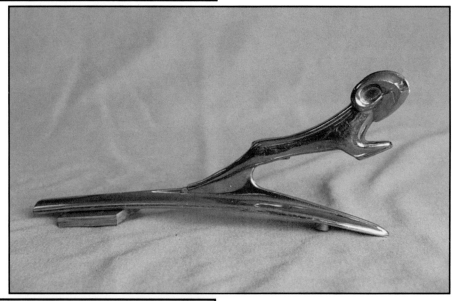

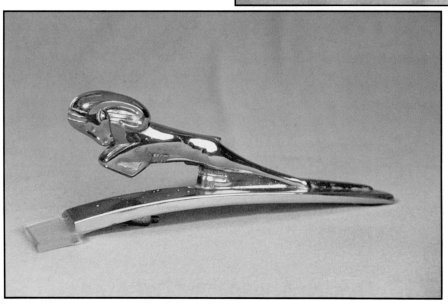

**YEAR:** 1938
**MODEL:** Dodge
**INF:** 589997
Truck

**#0238**

*U. S. Hood Ornaments and More . . .*

# DODGE

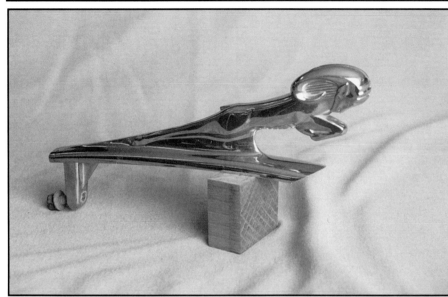

**YEAR:** 1939
**MODEL:** Dodge
**INF:** 788349 3711
Ram

**#0039**

**YEAR:** 1939
**MODEL:** Dodge
**INF:** 596175
Truck

**#0239**

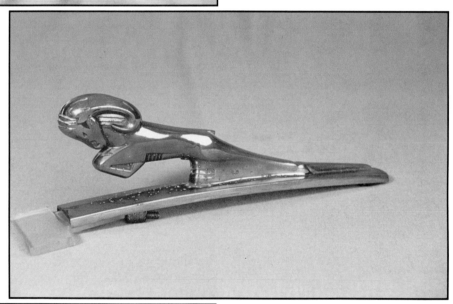

**YEAR:** 1940
**MODEL:** Dodge
**INF:** Buss H Series

**#0040**

U. S. Hood Ornaments and More . . .

## DODGE

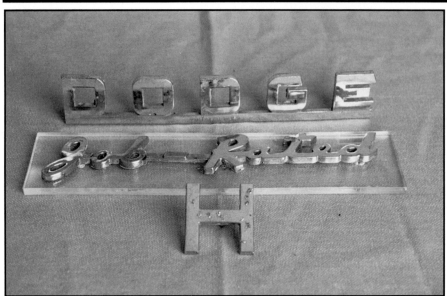

**YEAR:** 1940
**MODEL:** Dodge
**INF:** Job rated
1398730   1399941

**#0140**

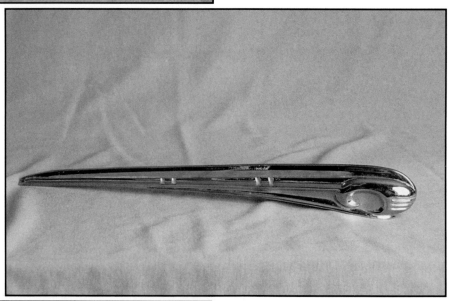

**YEAR:** 1941
**MODEL:** Dodge
**INF:** Ram

**#0041**

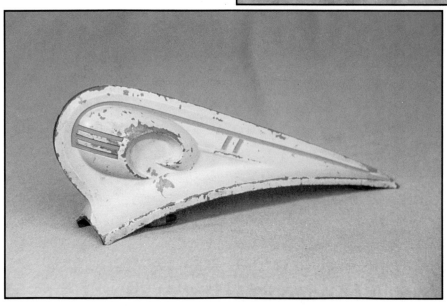

**YEAR:** 1941-1947
**MODEL:** Dodge
**INF:** 902973
Cab over truck

**#0141**

U. S. Hood Ornaments and More . . .

## DODGE

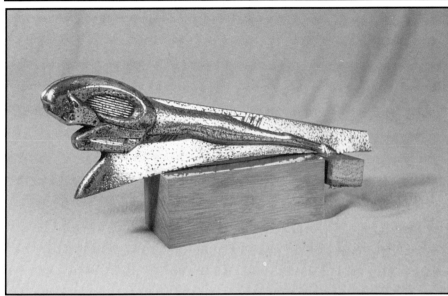

**YEAR:** 1942
**MODEL:** Dodge
**INF:** Similar to #46 but a thinner design

#0042

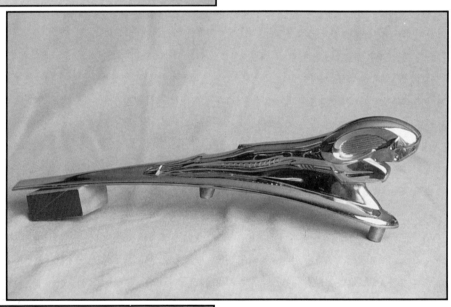

**YEAR:** 1946-1948
**MODEL:** Dodge
**INF:** 1158552

#0046

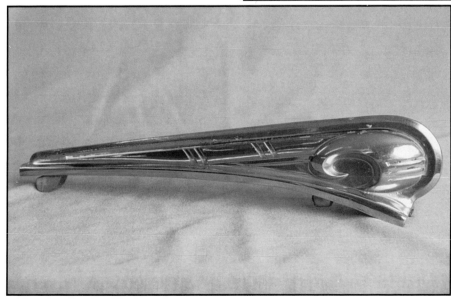

**YEAR:** 1947
**MODEL:** Dodge
**INF:** 913968 4626
Truck

#0047

U. S. Hood Ornaments and More . . .

## DODGE

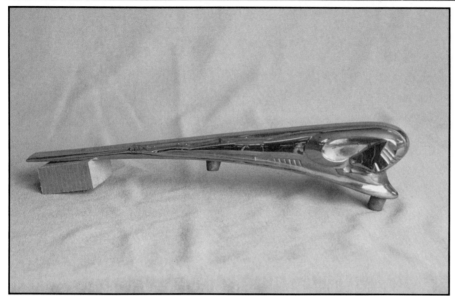

**YEAR:** 1946-1948
**MODEL:** Dodge
**INF:** 1148126
Ram

**#0048**

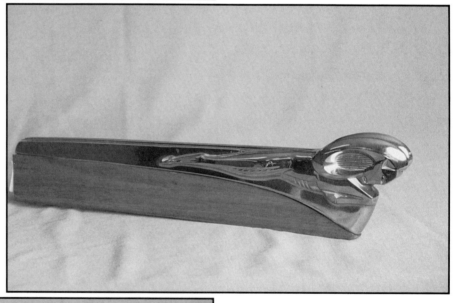

**YEAR:** 1948-1954
**MODEL:** Dodge
**INF:** 1097255
Truck

**#0148**

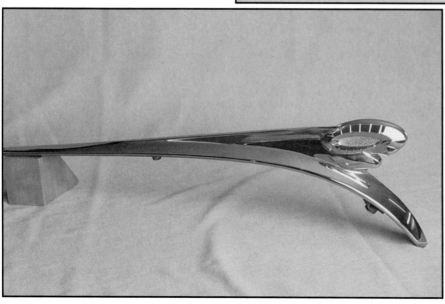

**YEAR:** 1949
**MODEL:** Dodge
**INF:** 1298935
Ram

**#0249**

U. S. Hood Ornaments and More . . .

# DODGE

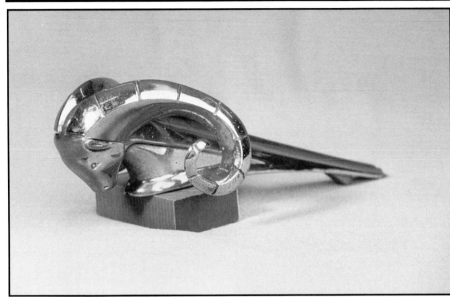

**YEAR:** 1951-1953
**MODEL:** Dodge
**INF:** Truck; larger nose & differently designed body

**#0051**

**YEAR:** 1952
**MODEL:** Dodge
**INF:** 1456355
1456356

**#0052**

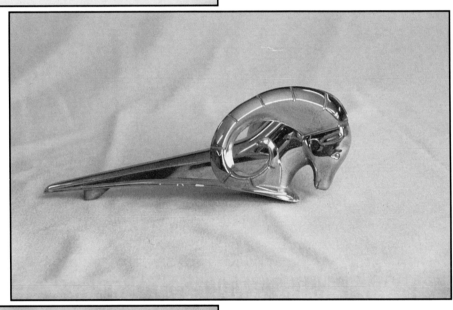

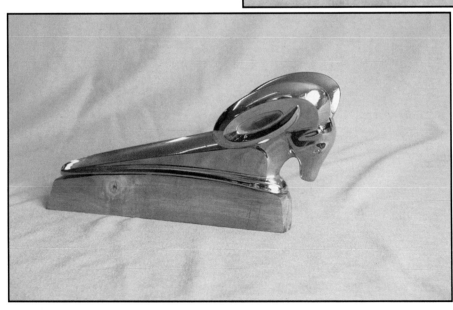

**YEAR:** 1953
**MODEL:** Dodge
**INF:** 1456250
Ram

**#0053**

U. S. Hood Ornaments and More . . .

# DODGE

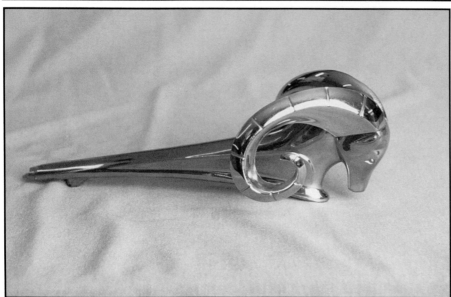

**YEAR:** 1953-1954
**MODEL:** Dodge
**INF:** 1456249
Ram

**#0153**

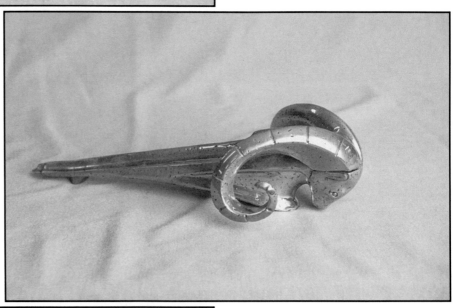

**YEAR:** 1953
**MODEL:** Dodge
**INF:** 1373215
Ram

**#0253**

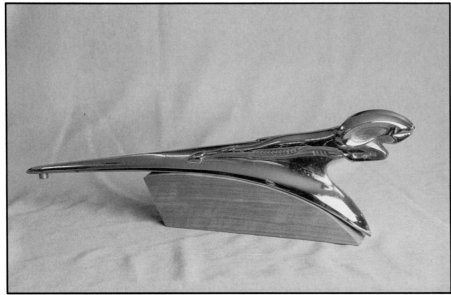

**YEAR:** 1954
**MODEL:** Dodge
**INF:** 1541101 9992
Ram

**#0054**

## DODGE

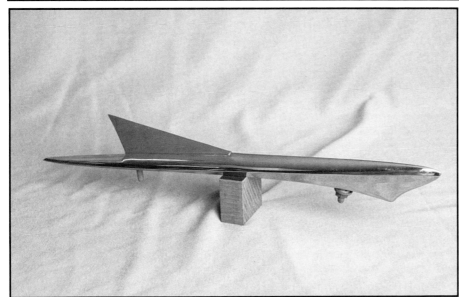

YEAR: 1957
MODEL: Dodge
INF: 16866330-1

#0057

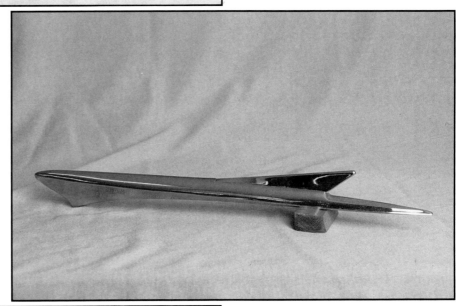

YEAR: 1958
MODEL: Dodge
INF: 1754502

#0058

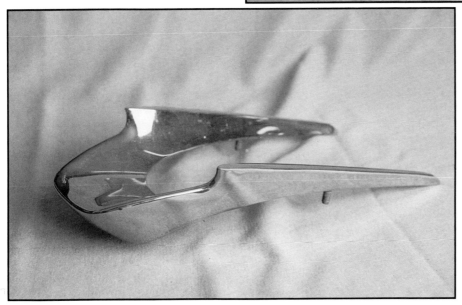

YEAR: 1959
MODEL: Dodge
INF: 1902673
Wing scoop

#0159

U. S. Hood Ornaments and More . . .

# DODGE

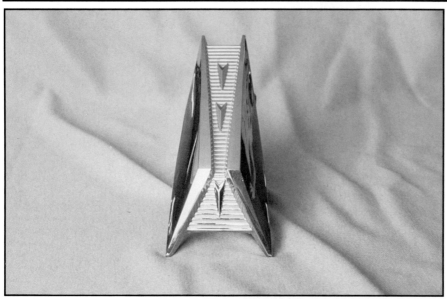

**YEAR:** 1960
**MODEL:** Dodge
**INF:** 1903477

#0060

**YEAR:** 1964
**MODEL:** Dodge
**INF:** 1903768
Hood emblem

#0064

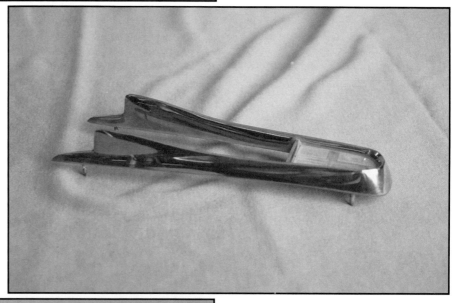

**YEAR:** 1978
**MODEL:** Dodge
**INF:** Le Baron
3868908

#0078

U. S. Hood Ornaments and More . . .

# DODGE

**YEAR:** 1980
**MODEL:** Dodge
**INF:** 12695 17405
Diplomat

**#0080**

**YEAR:** 1981
**MODEL:** Dodge
**INF:** 4103199
11744

**#0081**

**YEAR:** 1990
**MODEL:** Dodge
**INF:** Hood emblem

**#0090**

U. S. Hood Ornaments and More . . .

## DODGE

**YEAR:** 1990
**MODEL:** Dodge
**INF:** And Chrysler van

**#0190**

**YEAR:** 1990
**MODEL:** Dodge
**INF:** Truck

**#0290**

**YEAR:** 1990
**MODEL:** Dodge
**INF:** Truck; reproduction

**#0390**

## DODGE

**MODEL:** Dodge
**INF:** Charger script

**#0201**

**MODEL:** Dodge
**INF:** 2786-482 72270 2998-303 Dodge name

**#0202**

**MODEL:** Dodge
**INF:** Deluxe side emblem

**#0203**

## ESSEX

**YEAR:** 1928
**MODEL:** Essex
**INF:** Winged god
Pat. 767602

**#0028**

**YEAR:** 1935
**MODEL:** Essex
**INF:** Stylized eagle;
Terreplane 1 wing;
Hudson 2 wings

**#0035**

**YEAR:** 1935
**MODEL:** Essex
**INF:** Griffin Terraplane

**#0135**

U. S. Hood Ornaments and More . . .

# FORD

**YEAR:** 1932-1933
**MODEL:** Ford
**INF:** 40-18385
Greyhound

**#0033**

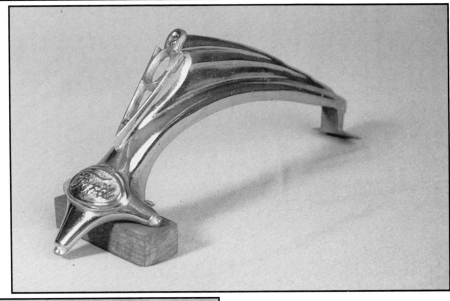

**YEAR:** 1934
**MODEL:** Ford
**INF:** 48-8215
V8 with chrome
Ford on front

**#0034**

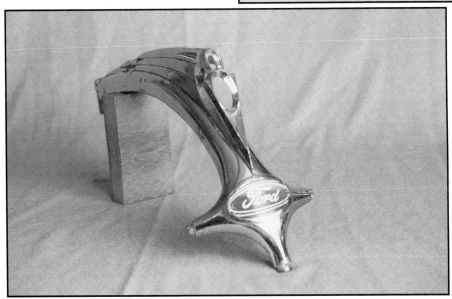

**YEAR:** 1935-1936
**MODEL:** Ford
**INF:** 68-8215
Model 69 51

**#0035**

# FORD

**YEAR:** 1935
**MODEL:** Ford
**INF:** Model; 50-51 commercial

**#0135**

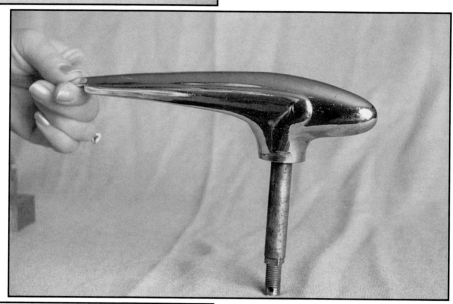

**YEAR:** 1936-1937
**MODEL:** Ford
**INF:** Latch & hood emblem

**#0037**

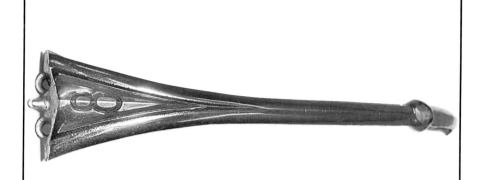

**YEAR:** 1938
**MODEL:** Ford
**INF:** 81A-8157B

**#0038**

U. S. Hood Ornaments and More . . .

# FORD

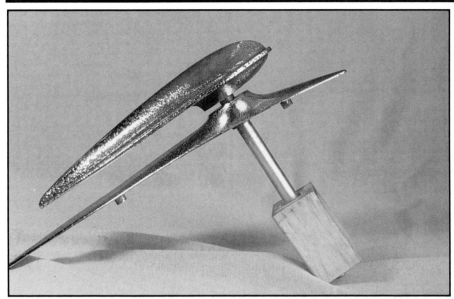

**YEAR:** 1938
**MODEL:** Ford
**INF:** Base 81-A
8218 A

#0138

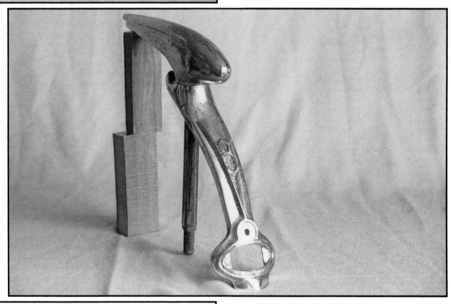

**YEAR:** 1938
**MODEL:** Ford
**INF:** Base 81-A 8218 A
and handle

#0238

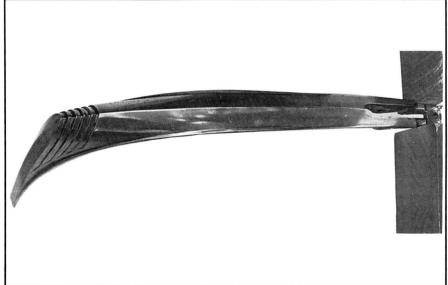

**YEAR:** 1939
**MODEL:** Ford
**INF:** 91A 8218 Deluxe
Front Ford with latch

#0039

U. S. Hood Ornaments and More . . .

# FORD

**YEAR:** 1940
**MODEL:** Ford
**INF:** 01A-8218A Standard
Ford vertical latch type

**#0040**

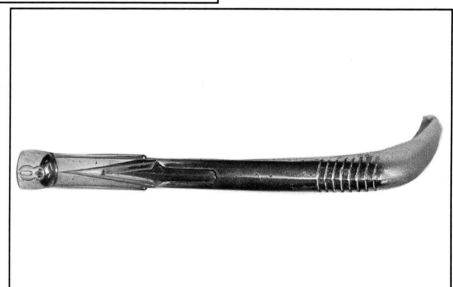

**YEAR:** 1940
**MODEL:** Ford
**INF:** 01A 8215 B Deluxe Front with latch 8

**#0140**

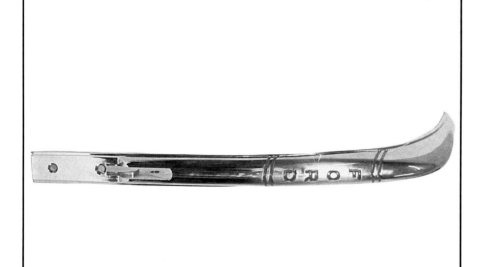

**YEAR:** 1940
**MODEL:** Ford
**INF:** OIC-8218
Vertical Ford; 2 hole

**#0240**

U. S. Hood Ornaments and More . . .

# FORD

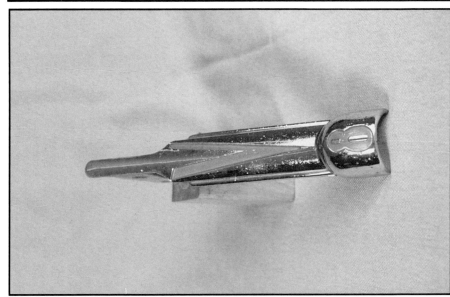

**YEAR:** 1940
**MODEL:** Ford
**INF:** 01A 8215-B
Latch

#0340

**YEAR:** 1946
**MODEL:** Ford
**INF:** 51A-16850
Styled wing with medalia 6

#0046

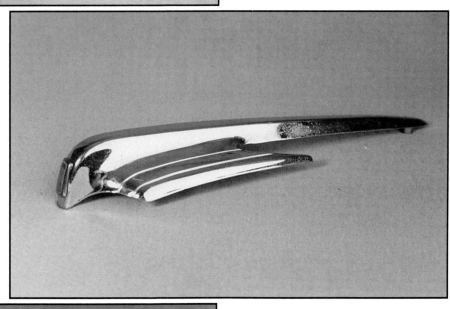

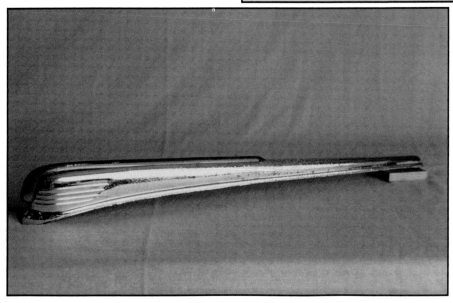

**YEAR:** 1948
**MODEL:** Ford
**INF:** 51A 16850
19" long; blue insert at top

#0048

*U. S. Hood Ornaments and More . . .*

## FORD

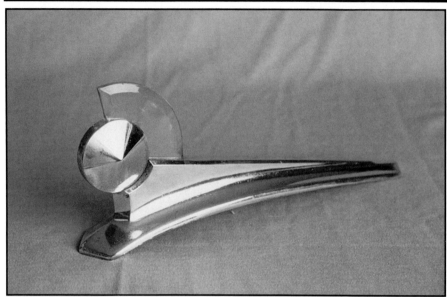

**YEAR:** 1949
**MODEL:** Ford
**INF:** 7981  8A-16650
11' long; 4-1/2" high

**#0049**

**YEAR:** 1949-1950
**MODEL:** Ford
**INF:** 0A-16851

**#0050**

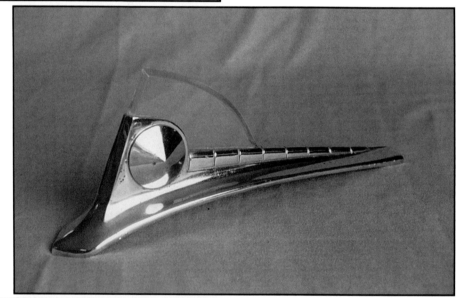

**YEAR:** 1951
**MODEL:** Ford
**INF:** A1-16851
0A-16852

**#0051**

## FORD

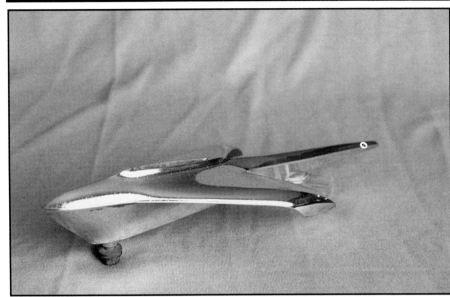

**YEAR:** 1952
**MODEL:** Ford
**INF:** 0A-16850
11-3/4" long

#0052

**YEAR:** 1953
**MODEL:** Ford
**INF:** BF-16850-1

#0053

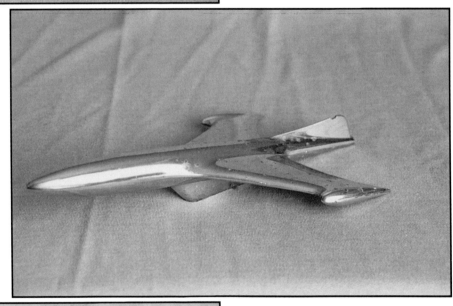

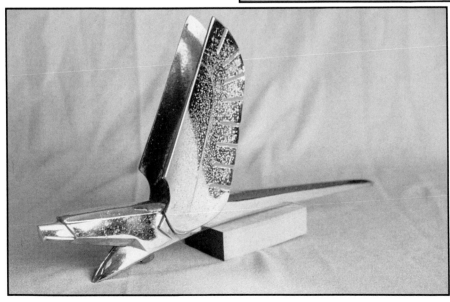

**YEAR:** 1953
**MODEL:** Ford
**INF:** BA 18244 B
Winged emblem

#0153

*U. S. Hood Ornaments and More . . .*

# FORD

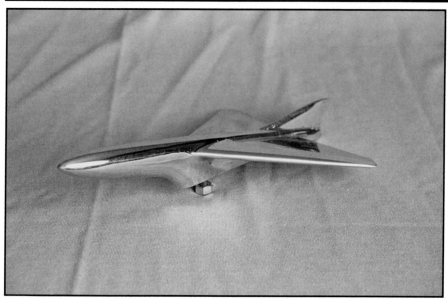

**YEAR:** 1954
**MODEL:** Ford
**INF:** BM16853-A

#0054

**YEAR:** 1954
**MODEL:** Ford
**INF:** 10677 LH
C4AB-16179-A

#0154

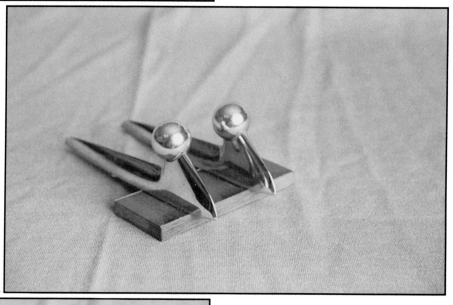

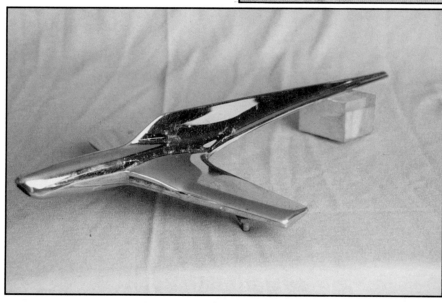

**YEAR:** 1955
**MODEL:** Ford
**INF:** BN-16853-C
Crown Victoria;
17-1/2" long;
10" wing span

#0055

## FORD

**YEAR:** 1955-1957
**MODEL:** Ford
**INF:** 800 Tractor 16600-A

**#0255**

**YEAR:** 1956
**MODEL:** Ford
**INF:** BJ-16868-A Fairlane

**#0056**

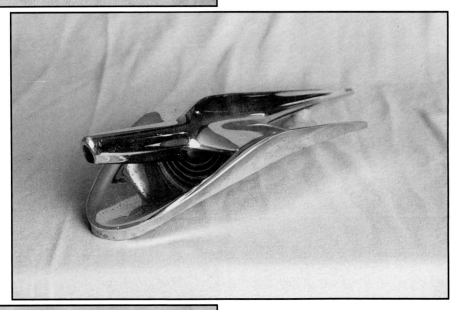

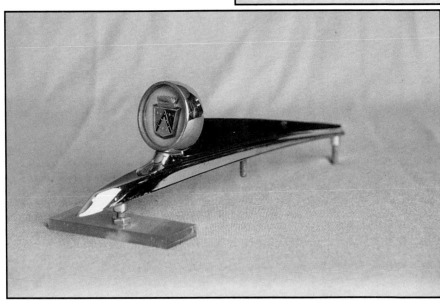

**YEAR:** 1957
**MODEL:** Ford
**INF:** BA1 16851-A Custom

**#0057**

U. S. Hood Ornaments and More . . .

# FORD

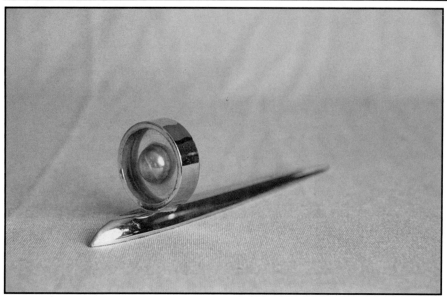

**YEAR:** 1958
**MODEL:** Ford
**INF:** BAP-18521B
25848-1

**#0058**

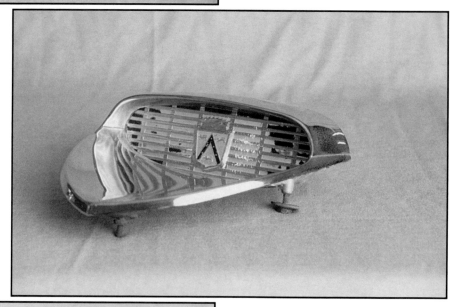

**YEAR:** 1958
**MODEL:** Ford
**INF:** BAD 16851-A
Hood scoop; Custom

**#0158**

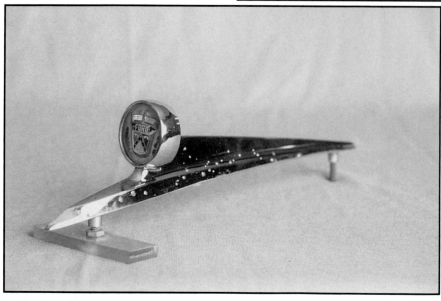

**YEAR:** 1959
**MODEL:** Ford
**INF:** BAC16853-A
Fairlane

**#0059**

U. S. Hood Ornaments and More . . .

# FORD

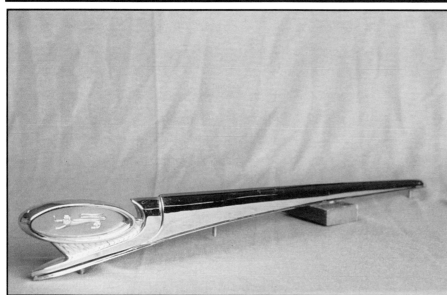

**YEAR:** 1960
**MODEL:** Ford
**INF:** COAB16905

**#0060**

**YEAR:** 1961
**MODEL:** Ford
**INF:** 16B224
16B225

**#0261**

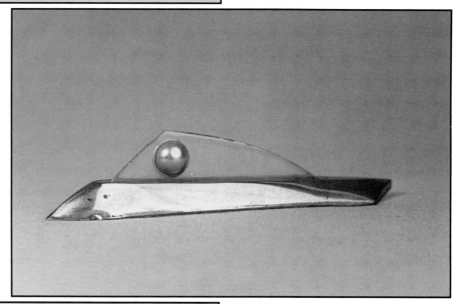

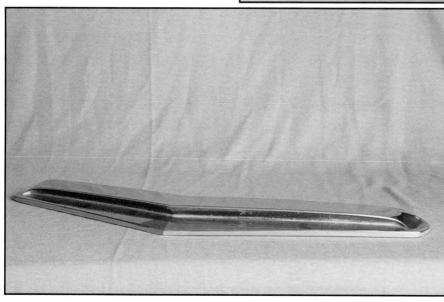

**YEAR:** 1962
**MODEL:** Ford
**INF:** C2DB 16607-A
Falcon

**#0062**

U. S. Hood Ornaments and More . . .

# FORD

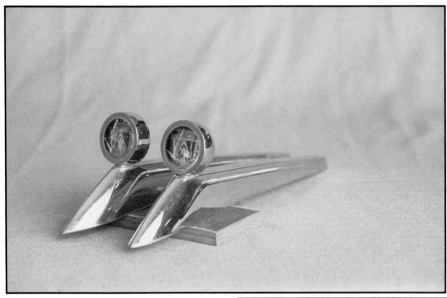

**YEAR:** 1962
**MODEL:** Ford
**INF:** C2AB-16A105-A LH
C2AB-16A104-A   RH
Falcon

**#0162**

**YEAR:** 1962
**MODEL:** Ford
**INF:** C2AB 16B225 B LH
C2AB 16B226 B   RH

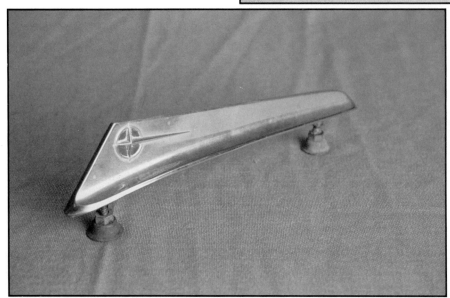

**YEAR:** 1963
**MODEL:** Ford
**INF:** C30B-16A101-A
Fairlane

**#0063**

U. S. Hood Ornaments and More . . .

# FORD

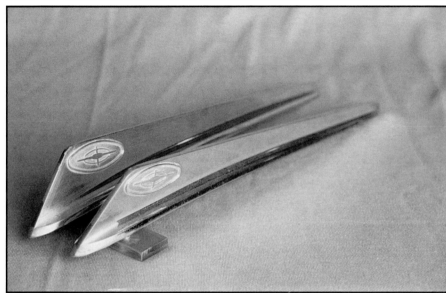

**YEAR:** 1963
**MODEL:** Ford
**INF:** C2AB-16225 LH
C2AB-16224 RH
500

#0163

**YEAR:** 1964
**MODEL:** Ford
**INF:** C4AB-16178-A
C4AB-16179-A   Fender

#0064

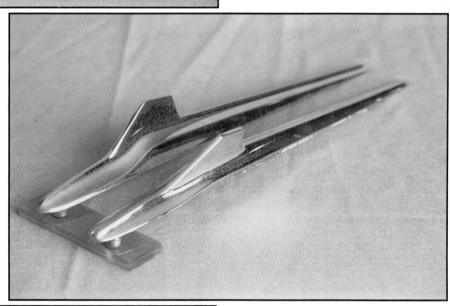

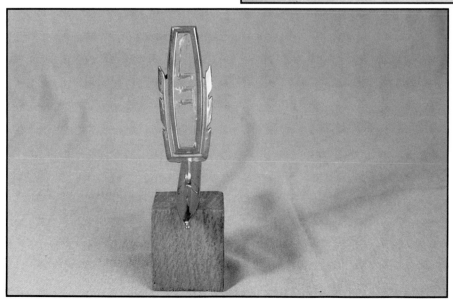

**YEAR:** 1967
**MODEL:** Ford
**INF:** D4EB 8343 AA
Elite

#0067

*U. S. Hood Ornaments and More . . .*

# FORD

**YEAR:** 1975
**MODEL:** Ford
**INF:** Truck Explorer D5TB

**#0075**

**YEAR:** 1977
**MODEL:** Ford
**INF:** D70B 8B343-AA LTD

**#0077**

**YEAR:** 1978
**MODEL:** Ford
**INF:** Granada D8DB8B523 AA

**#0078**

U. S. Hood Ornaments and More . . .

# FORD

**YEAR:** 1958
**MODEL:** Ford Edsel
**INF:** Ranger

**#0058**

**YEAR:** 1959
**MODEL:** Ford Edsel
**INF:** 1018271 69069
1018270 69068 Fender

**#0059**

**YEAR:** 1955
**MODEL:** Ford T Bird
**INF:** Nose assembly

**#0155**

U. S. Hood Ornaments and More . . .

# FORD

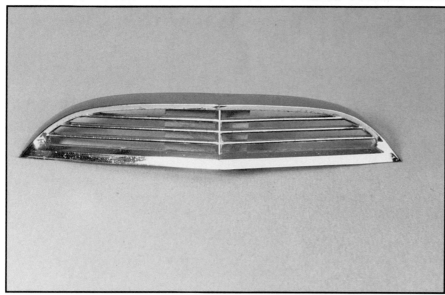

**YEAR:** 1955-1956
**MODEL:** Ford T Bird
**INF:** Air scoop

#0156

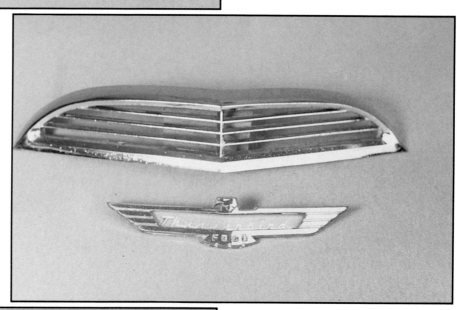

**YEAR:** 1956-1957
**MODEL:** Ford T Bird
**INF:** BAB 88392-B
Scoop and emblem

#0157

**YEAR:** 1959
**MODEL:** Ford T Bird
**INF:** B9SB16A046
PT10402
Fender emblem

#0259

U. S. Hood Ornaments and More . . .

# FORD

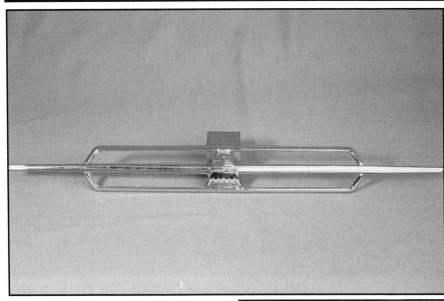

**YEAR:** 1966
**MODEL:** Ford T Bird
**INF:** Rear
C6A B 13616

#0166

**YEAR:** 1978
**MODEL:** Ford T Bird
**INF:** D7SB8B343 BA
Hood emblem

#0178

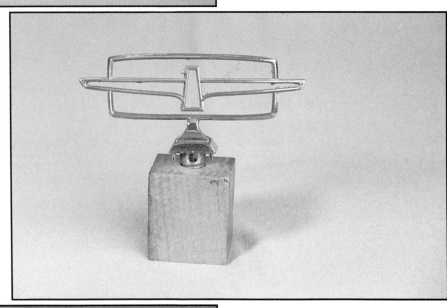

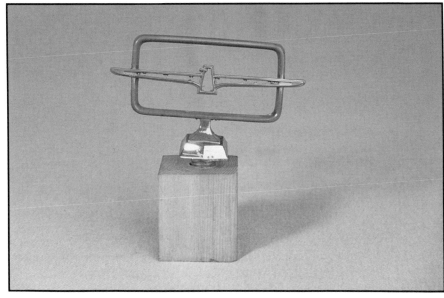

**YEAR:** 1981
**MODEL:** Ford T Bird
**INF:** EO5B8C085-AA
Hood emblem

#0080

U. S. Hood Ornaments and More . . .

# FORD

**MODEL:** Ford T Bird
**INF:** C5SB 63291 A 36A

#0340

**MODEL:** Ford T Bird
**INF:** C3SB 63231 A1 36A

#0341

**MODEL:** Ford T Bird
**INF:** BAA 402 5622-A Script

#0342

U. S. Hood Ornaments and More . . .

# FORD

**MODEL:** Ford
**INF:** 16721 A LH
F-250 side plate

**#0301**

**MODEL:** Ford
**INF:** Crestliner RH

**#0302**

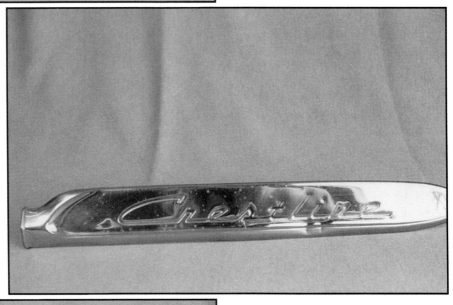

**MODEL:** Ford
**INF:** C9AB 5429
Galaxie

**#0303**

*U. S. Hood Ornaments and More . . .*

# FORD

**MODEL:** Ford
**INF:** C7GB 16098-A
KBC 24717 LH
Cyclone

#0304

**MODEL:** Ford
**INF:** 500

#0305

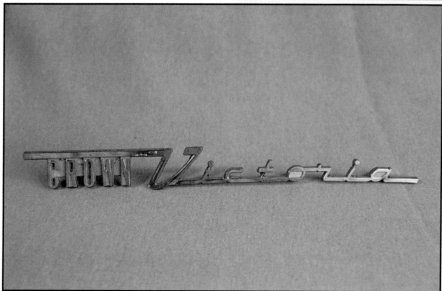

**MODEL:** Ford
**INF:** BN 6425622 10545
Crown Victoria

#0306

## FORD

**MODEL:** Ford
**INF:** C4ZB 16098-0
Mustang

#0307

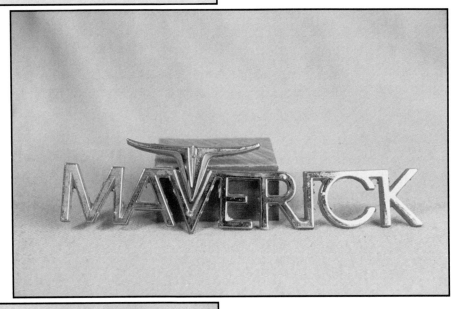

**MODEL:** Ford
**INF:** DODB 16098-8
Maverick

#0308

**MODEL:** Ford
**INF:** C9ZB 16098-A
Mustang

#0309

# FORD

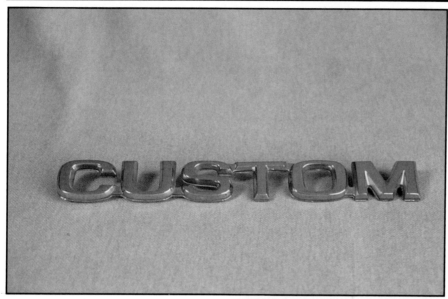

**MODEL:** Ford
**INF:** E0TB 16B114-C
Custom

#0310

**MODEL:** Ford
**INF:** C50B 16093-A
Fairlane

#0311

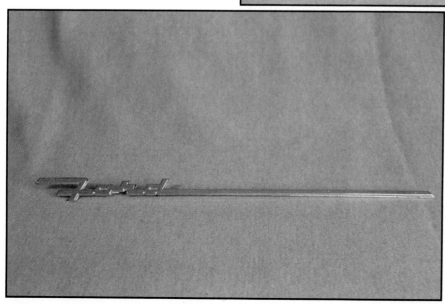

**MODEL:** Ford
**INF:** BN700-4460-A
Ford

#0312

U. S. Hood Ornaments and More . . .

# FORD

**MODEL:** Ford
**INF:** C6DB 16098 LH
Futura

#0313

**MODEL:** Ford
**INF:** BM 16237-A
V8 Emblem

#0314

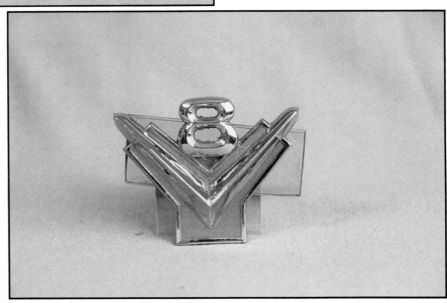

**MODEL:** Ford
**INF:** C8ZB 16C228-D  LH
Mustang 289 side emblem

#0315

U. S. Hood Ornaments and More . . .

# FORD

**MODEL:** Ford
**INF:** BAC 16098 A
Script; Ranchero

#0316

**MODEL:** Ford
**INF:** Custom

#0317

**MODEL:** Ford
**INF:** Ranchero

#0318

U. S. Hood Ornaments and More . . .

# FORD

**MODEL:** Ford
**INF:** C3AB 160179-B
500 XL Galaxie

#0319

**MODEL:** Ford
**INF:** 62291A36-A
Falcon script

#0320

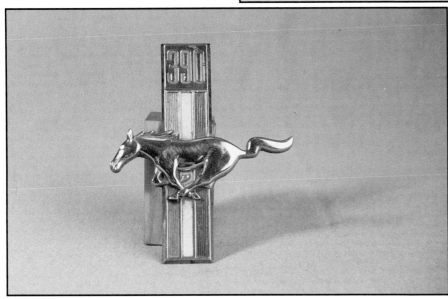

**MODEL:** Ford
**INF:** Must C7ZB-16C228B
1 PR; 1967
390 Mustang side shields

#0321

U. S. Hood Ornaments and More . . .

## FORD

**MODEL:** Ford
**INF:** Mustang
C8ZB 8A224;
1968

**#0322**

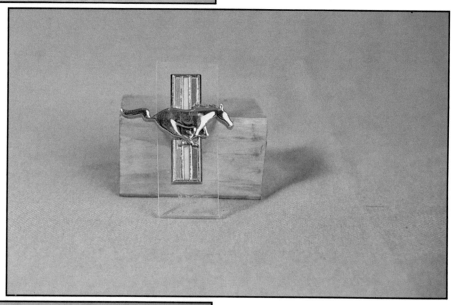

**MODEL:** Ford
**INF:** Mustang
C9ZB 6520803;
1968; 1 pr.

**#0323**

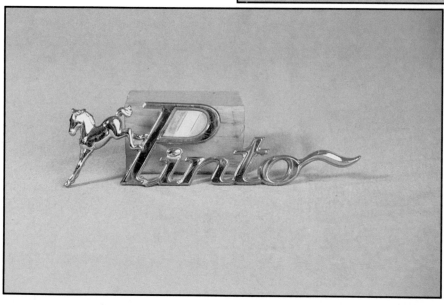

**MODEL:** Ford
**INF:** Pinto
16B114 AD; 1970
Pinto with name

**#0324**

U. S. Hood Ornaments and More . . .

# FORD

**MODEL:** Ford
**INF:** Mustang
D4ZB 8216-AA; 1974
Front mustang

#0325

**MODEL:** Ford
**INF:** 85 HP
Truck side emblems;
1937

#0326

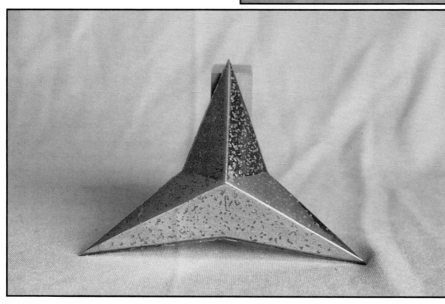

**MODEL:** Ford
**INF:** BAAA-8259-D
Truck; 1953; star

#0327

*U. S. Hood Ornaments and More . . .*

# FORD

**MODEL:** Ford
**INF:** CO7B16720 RH; 1954; F-100 side hood

#0328

**MODEL:** Ford
**INF:** BAAA16637-A
Truck

#0329

**MODEL:** Ford
**INF:** 1946; 51A8259
Front end

#0330

U. S. Hood Ornaments and More . . .

# FORD

**MODEL:** Ford
**INF:** Aftermarket wings; 1954

#0331

**MODEL:** Ford
**INF:** F100 Truck C4TB16607-A; 1964

#0332

**MODEL:** Ford
**INF:** Super van C8AB-8940412 A

#0333

U. S. Hood Ornaments and More . . .

# FORD

**MODEL:** Ford
**INF:** Maverick
D0D-6242550

**#0334**

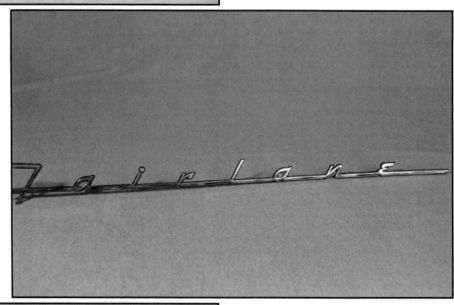

**MODEL:** Ford
**INF:** Fairlane script
AC 16098

**#0335**

**MODEL:** Ford
**INF:** Granada gas cap; 1975

**#0336**

U. S. Hood Ornaments and More . . .

# FORD

**MODEL:** Ford
**INF:** C76B-16098-A
Cyclone

#0337

**MODEL:** Ford
**INF:** C3TB 16A652-A
750 Truck

#0338

**MODEL:** Ford
**INF:** D3AB 142514 AB

#0339

U. S. Hood Ornaments and More . . .

## GENERAL MOTORS CORPORATION

**YEAR:** 1930
**MODEL:** GMC
**INF:** Oval, brass GMC cap

**#0030**

**YEAR:** 1948-1954
**MODEL:** GMC
**INF:** 2233301-1 Jet; drooped wings with pods; on hood bracket

**#0048**

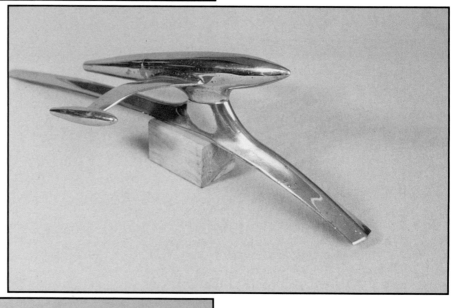

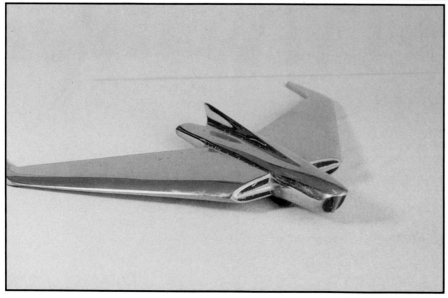

**YEAR:** 1955-1957
**MODEL:** GMC
**INF:** Large swept back wings with 2 tail engines

**#0055**

U. S. Hood Ornaments and More . . .

# GRAHAM

**YEAR:** 1937
**MODEL:** Graham
**INF:** Crusader 85

**#0037**

**YEAR:** 1938-1939
**MODEL:** Graham
**INF:** C207074
Brown insert; hood latch and emblem

**#0038**

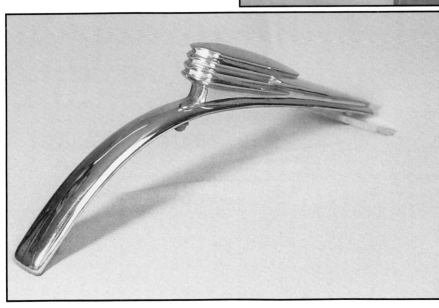

**YEAR:** 1940
**MODEL:** Graham
**INF:** 5752
Hood emblem

**#0040**

U. S. Hood Ornaments and More . . .

# HUDSON

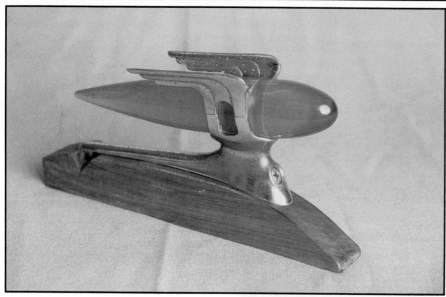

**YEAR:** 1933-1944
**MODEL:** Hudson
**INF:** Terraplane;
red torpedo

**#0033**

**YEAR:** 1935
**MODEL:** Hudson
**INF:** 2 winged for 6 cylinder

**#0035**

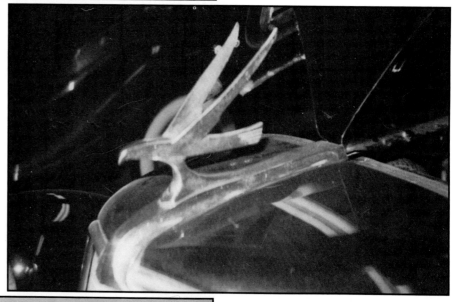

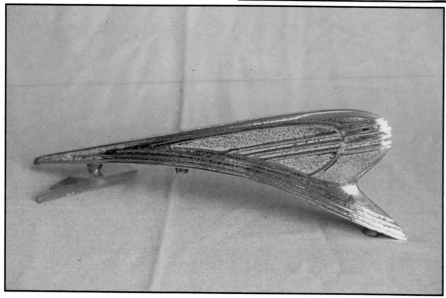

**YEAR:** 1939
**MODEL:** Hudson
**INF:** 134158 90 98

**#0039**

## HUDSON

**YEAR:** 1940
**MODEL:** Hudson
**INF:** 7791
Small chrome arch; 11" long

**#0040**

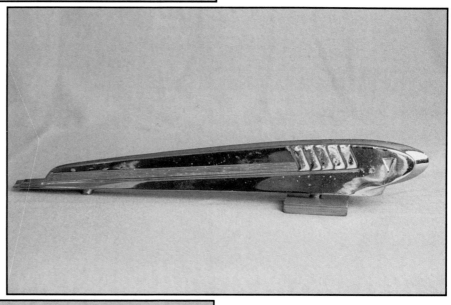

**YEAR:** 1946-1947
**MODEL:** Hudson
**INF:** 208768-208769
6 & 8 cylinder; plain

**#0046**

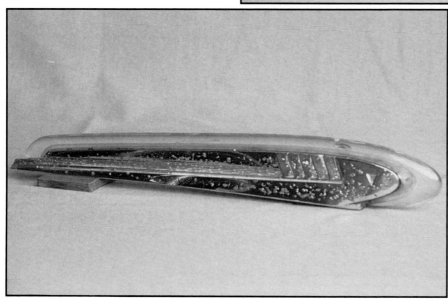

**YEAR:** 1946-1947
**MODEL:** Hudson
**INF:** 208768-208769
Plastic top;
Commodore 6 & 8 cylinder

**#0146**

U. S. Hood Ornaments and More . . .

# HUDSON

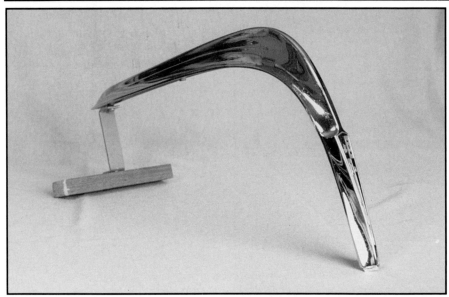

**YEAR:** 1946-1947
**MODEL:** Hudson
**INF:** 140870 4760

**#0246**

**YEAR:** 1948-1949
**MODEL:** Hudson
**INF:** 210816
Commodore 6 & 8 cylinder; fender

**#0048**

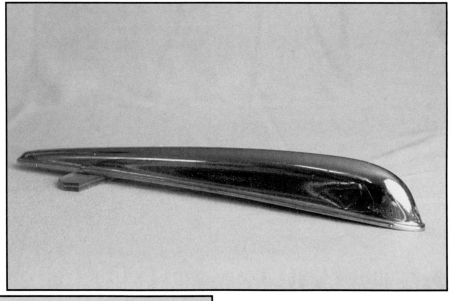

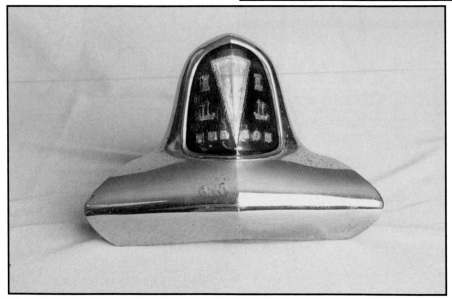

**YEAR:** 1948-1949
**MODEL:** Hudson
**INF:** 211512 7761

**#0148**

*U. S. Hood Ornaments and More . . .*

## HUDSON

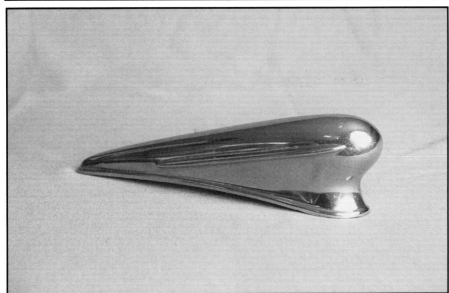

**YEAR:** 1948-1949
**MODEL:** Hudson
**INF:** 210645  418733
Super 6 & 8 cylinder

#0049

**YEAR:** 1950-1951
**MODEL:** Hudson
**INF:** 220346
Medium silver arch

#0050

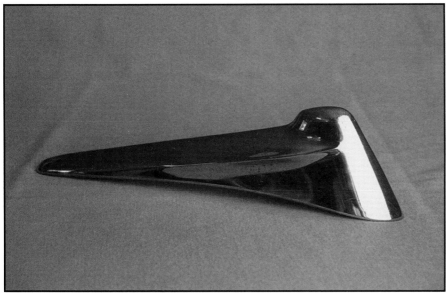

**YEAR:** 1950-1951
**MODEL:** Hudson
**INF:** 233055  8548
Pacer

#0150

U. S. Hood Ornaments and More . . .

# HUDSON

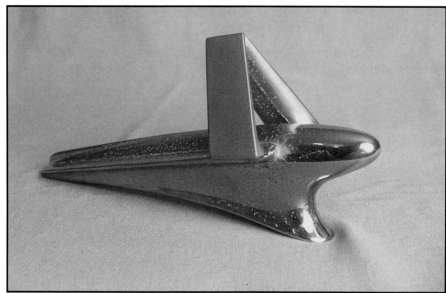

**YEAR:** 1951
**MODEL:** Hudson
**INF:** 220346 8548
Commercial Wasp

**#0051**

**YEAR:** 1951
**MODEL:** Hudson
**INF:** 220846 210641
Hornet

**#0151**

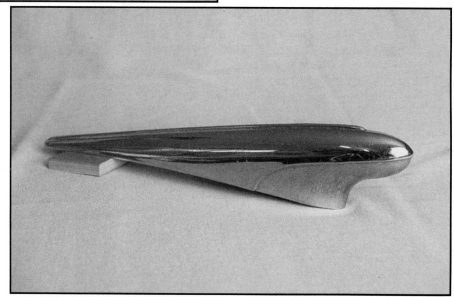

**YEAR:** 1952
**MODEL:** Hudson
**INF:** Hornet
230622

**#0052**

## HUDSON

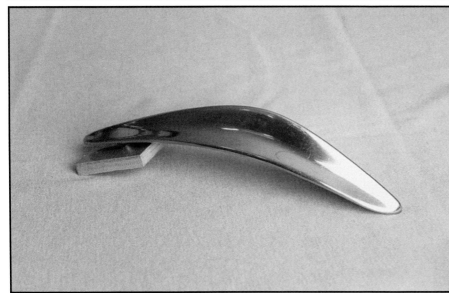

**YEAR:** 1952
**MODEL:** Hudson
**INF:** Pacemaker
230612

**#0152**

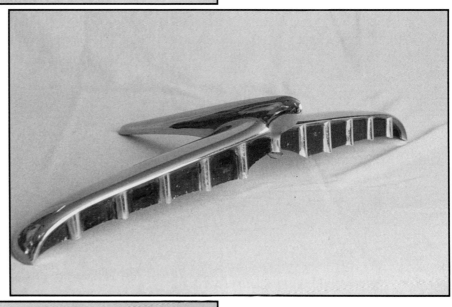

**YEAR:** 1953-1954
**MODEL:** Hudson
**INF:** 238425 22077
Hornet/Wasp

**#0053**

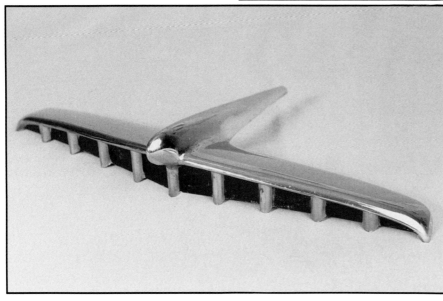

**YEAR:** 1953-1954
**MODEL:** Hudson
**INF:** Jet
285810 22019

**#0153**

U. S. Hood Ornaments and More . . .

## HUDSON

**YEAR:** 1954
**MODEL:** Hudson
**INF:** Center #240893
Hornet—personal car;
2 piece ornament;
14-1/2" long; approx.
25" wide

**#0054**

**YEAR:** 1955
**MODEL:** Hudson
**INF:** Wasp 3118490
Gold front trim

**#0055**

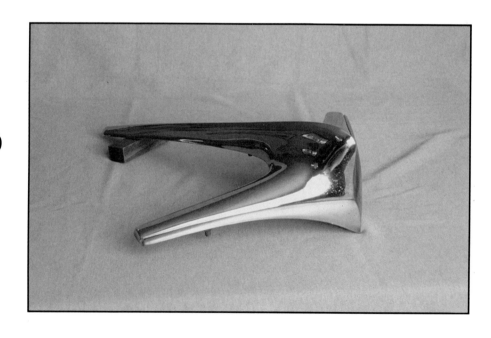

U. S. Hood Ornaments and More . . .

# HUDSON

**MODEL:** Hudson
**INF:** 211170 9902
Script

#0901

**MODEL:** Hudson
**INF:** Plastic script

#0902

*U. S. Hood Ornaments and More . . .*

# INTERNATIONAL HARVESTER COMPANY

**YEAR:** 1937
**MODEL:** IHC
**INF:** 3 diamonds;
1 blue & 2 white

#0037

**YEAR:** 1946-1948
**MODEL:** IHC
**INF:** 61739-1
Chrome front

#0046

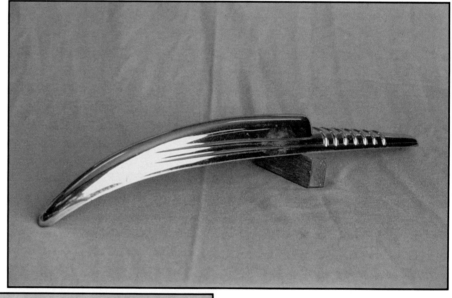

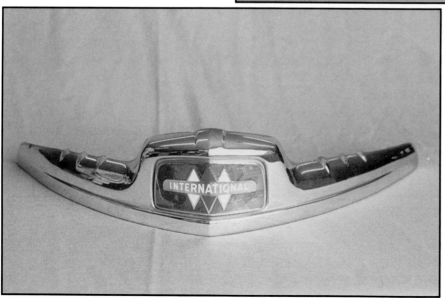

**YEAR:** 1946-1949
**MODEL:** IHC
**INF:** 61741-R1

#0048

## KAISER

**YEAR:** 1949
**MODEL:** Kaiser
**INF:** 754461 8373
17" long; 6" high;
Frazer

**#0049**

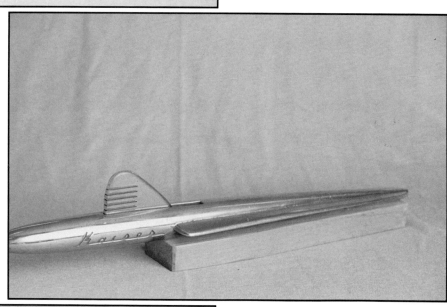

**YEAR:** 1950
**MODEL:** Kaiser
**INF:** Plastic fin with name

**#0050**

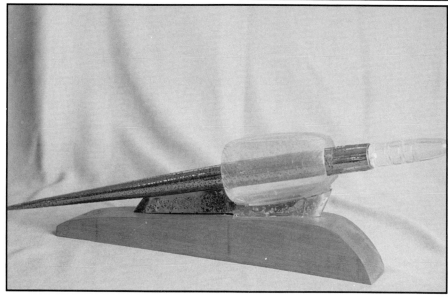

**YEAR:** 1951
**MODEL:** Kaiser
**INF:** Spear with plastic cover sleeve

**#0051**

*U. S. Hood Ornaments and More . . .*

# KAISER

**YEAR:** 1953
**MODEL:** Kaiser
**INF:** Henry J.'s personal car

**#0053**

**YEAR:** 1953
**MODEL:** Kaiser
**INF:** 793039

**#0153**

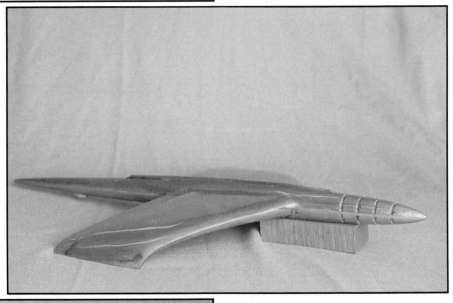

**YEAR:** 1953
**MODEL:** Kaiser
**INF:** 791978

**#0253**

U. S. Hood Ornaments and More . . .

# KAISER

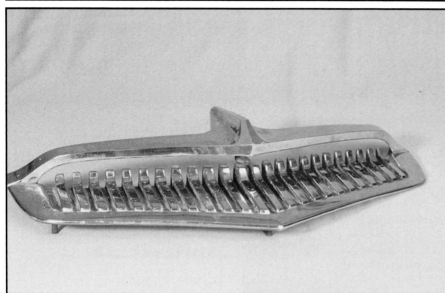

**YEAR:** 1955
**MODEL:** Kaiser
**INF:** 794153  9890
794154  9892

**#0055**

**MODEL:** Kaiser
**INF:** 792753  9525
Script

**#0701**

**MODEL:** Kaiser
**INF:** 9526  792754
Manhattan script

**#0702**

U. S. Hood Ornaments and More . . .

# LAFAYETTE

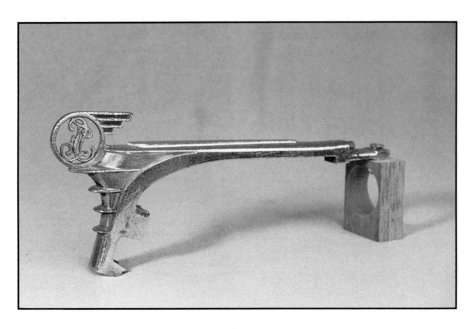

**YEAR:** 1935-1936
**MODEL:** LaFayette
**INF:** 4088
LF in circle

**#0136**

*U. S. Hood Ornaments and More . . .*

# LINCOLN

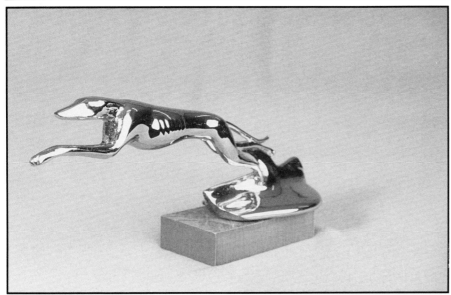

**YEAR:** 1927-1933
**MODEL:** Lincoln
**INF:** Small neck cap

**#0027**

**YEAR:** 1934-1937
**MODEL:** Lincoln
**INF:** Greyhound

**#0034**

**YEAR:** 1937
**MODEL:** Lincoln
**INF:** Hood latch as well as emblem

**#0037**

U. S. Hood Ornaments and More . . .

# LINCOLN

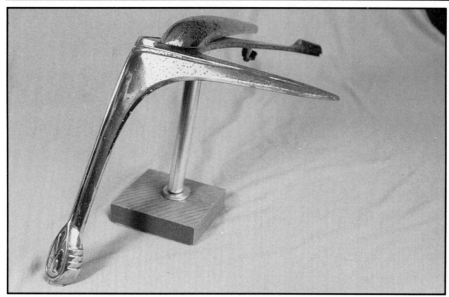

**YEAR:** 1940
**MODEL:** Lincoln
**INF:** Zephyr
06H 16624; 06H 16776
Hood release and ornament

#0040

**YEAR:** 1940-1948
**MODEL:** Lincoln
**INF:** Gold ball & spear

#0041

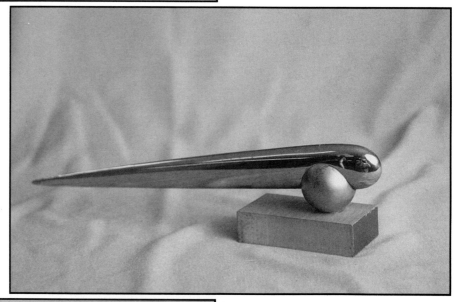

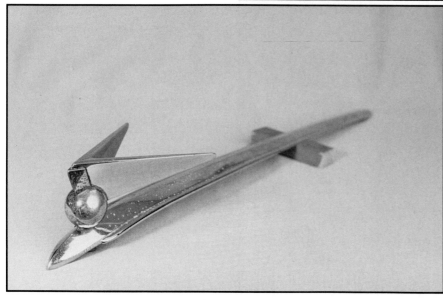

**YEAR:** 1942-1948
**MODEL:** Lincoln
**INF:** 26H 16776
Hood base with winged ball

#0042

U. S. Hood Ornaments and More . . .

# LINCOLN

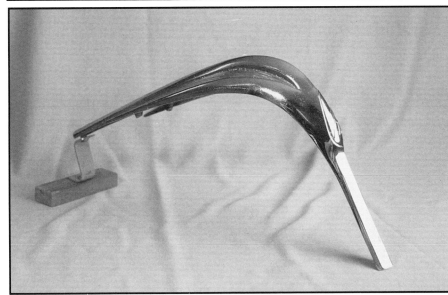

**YEAR:** 1944
**MODEL:** Lincoln
**INF:** Zephyr
16H 16852

**#0044**

**YEAR:** 1949-1950
**MODEL:** Lincoln
**INF:** Gold underswept wings

**#0049**

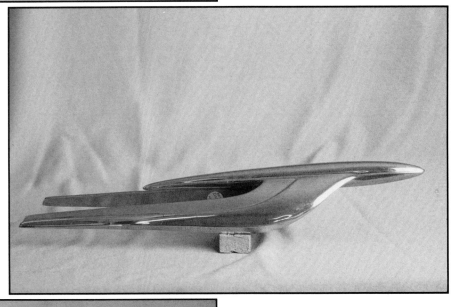

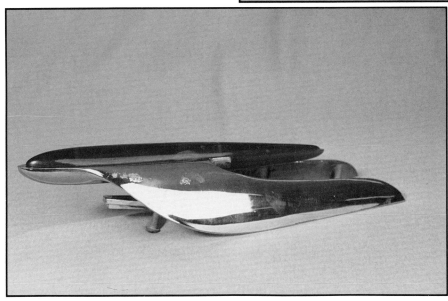

**YEAR:** 1949-1953
**MODEL:** Lincoln
**INF:** Aftermarket Lincoln and Mercury

**#0149**

U. S. Hood Ornaments and More . . .

## LINCOLN

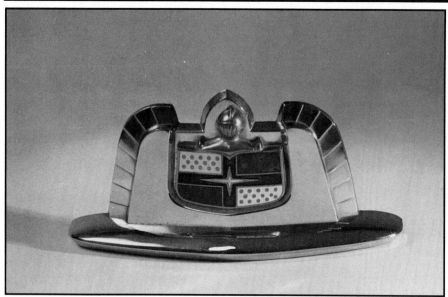

**YEAR:** 1950-1951
**MODEL:** Lincoln
**INF:** 0L-16644
Hood emblem

**#0050**

**YEAR:** 1951
**MODEL:** Lincoln
**INF:** 16852- Base
IL 16853 - Gold spear

**#0051**

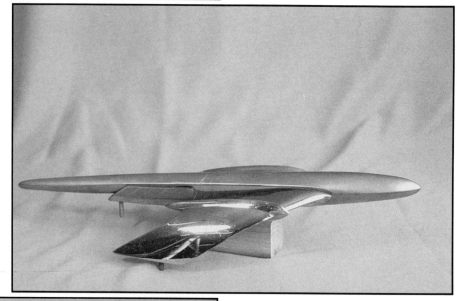

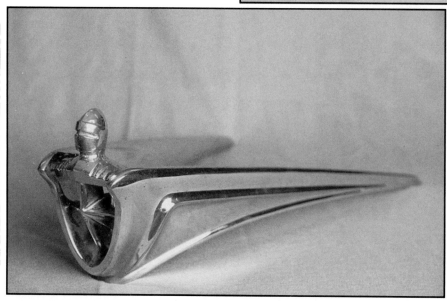

**YEAR:** 1955-1956
**MODEL:** Lincoln
**INF:** BY-16868
10680

**#0055**

*U. S. Hood Ornaments and More . . .*

## LINCOLN

**YEAR:** 1957
**MODEL:** Lincoln
**INF:** XO-1235

**#0057**

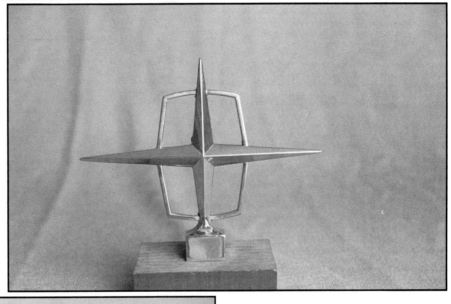

**YEAR:** 1961-1964
**MODEL:** Lincoln
**INF:** Extreme slope on base

**#0061**

**YEAR:** 1965-1966
**MODEL:** Lincoln
**INF:** Minimum slope on base

**#0065**

U. S. Hood Ornaments and More . . .

# LINCOLN

**YEAR:** 1967
**MODEL:** Lincoln
**INF:** EOVR 8C078

#0067

**MODEL:** Lincoln
**INF:** 1949 trunk cover

#0701

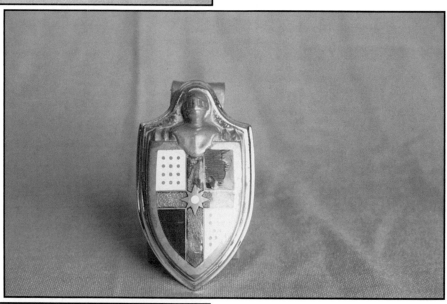

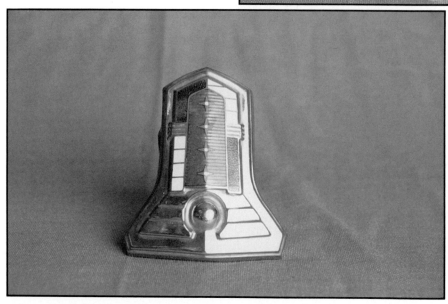

**MODEL:** Lincoln
**INF:** Shield; 1951

#0702

U. S. Hood Ornaments and More . . .

# MACK

**YEAR:** 1932
**MODEL:** Mack
**INF:** Pat. 87931
1932 & up truck

#0032

**MODEL:** Mack
**INF:** 27RU247
Truck bulldog

#0050

U. S. Hood Ornaments and More . . .

# MERCURY

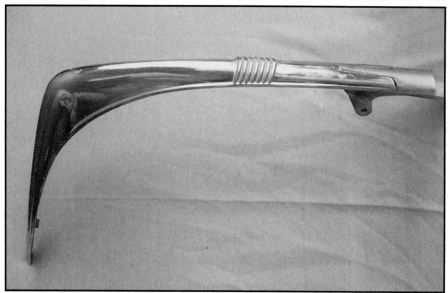

**YEAR:** 1939
**MODEL:** Mercury
**INF:** Top and front opener ornament; 218

#0039

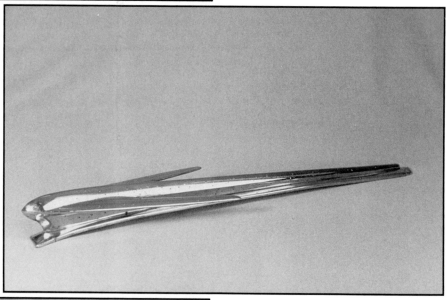

**YEAR:** 1941
**MODEL:** Mercury
**INF:** 19A 18389

#0041

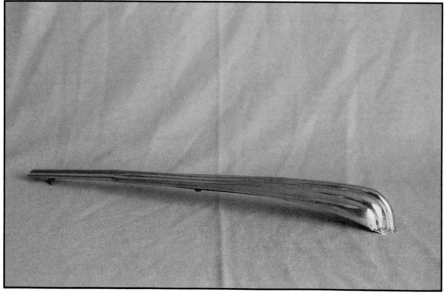

**YEAR:** 1942
**MODEL:** Mercury
**INF:** 29A 16850
Stamped steel

#0042

U. S. Hood Ornaments and More . . .

# MERCURY

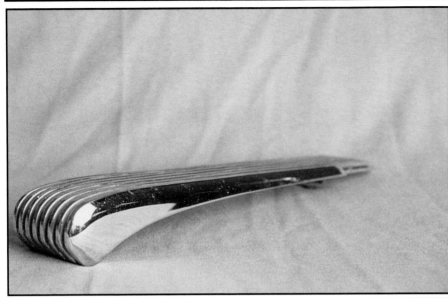

**YEAR:** 1946
**MODEL:** Mercury
**INF:** A 16850

#0046

**YEAR:** 1949
**MODEL:** Mercury
**INF:** BR16851 9848
Stamped steel

#0049

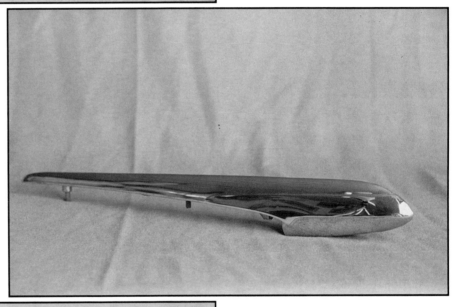

**YEAR:** 1950
**MODEL:** Mercury
**INF:** C88A-16850
Monarch Canadian

#0050

U. S. Hood Ornaments and More . . .

## MERCURY

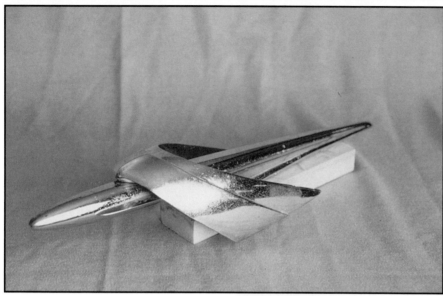

**YEAR:** 1950-1951
**MODEL:** Mercury
**INF:** 8N16850 (49-51)
0M16850 (50-51)

#0150

**YEAR:** 1951
**MODEL:** Mercury
**INF:** IM 16637
Center to tip 19-1/2";
over all 37"

#0051

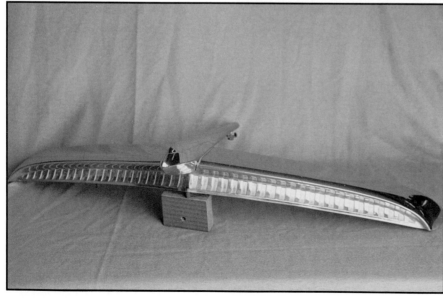

**YEAR:** 1954
**MODEL:** Mercury
**INF:** 16851 9848-1

#0054

U. S. Hood Ornaments and More . . .

# MERCURY

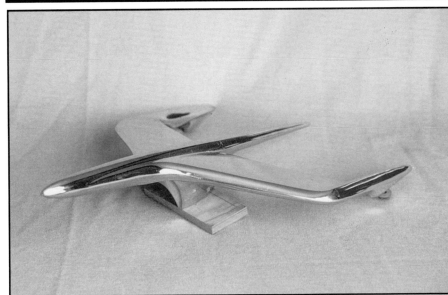

**YEAR:** 1955
**MODEL:** Mercury
**INF:** BV16850B
10460

#0155

**YEAR:** 1956
**MODEL:** Mercury
**INF:** XD 1173

#0056

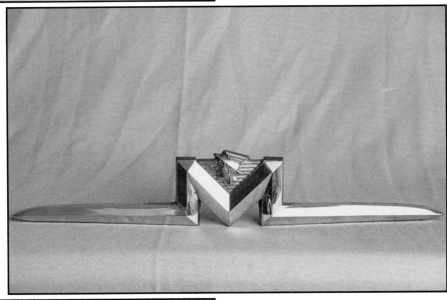

**YEAR:** 1957
**MODEL:** Mercury
**INF:** BAE 16853A
X01422

#0057

U. S. Hood Ornaments and More . . .

## MERCURY

**YEAR:** 1958-1959
**MODEL:** Mercury
**INF:** One pair fender emblems; 17314

**#0058**

**YEAR:** 1961
**MODEL:** Mercury
**INF:** 28073-311 28072-311 Fender CIKB-16A208B & 16A290

**#0061**

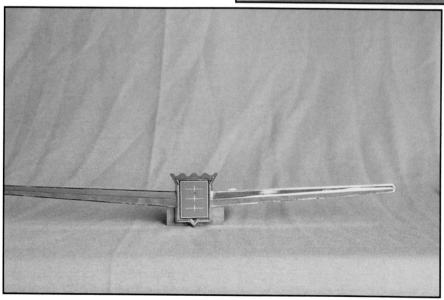

**YEAR:** 1967
**MODEL:** Mercury
**INF:** C7MB-8B362-A 15427

**#0067**

U. S. Hood Ornaments and More . . .

# MERCURY

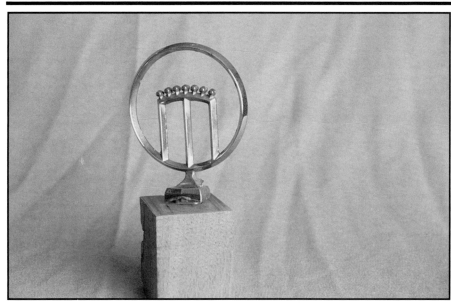

**YEAR:** 1969
**MODEL:** Mercury
**INF:** Grand Marquis

**#0069**

**YEAR:** 1969
**MODEL:** Mercury
**INF:** 3691540
55062

**#0169**

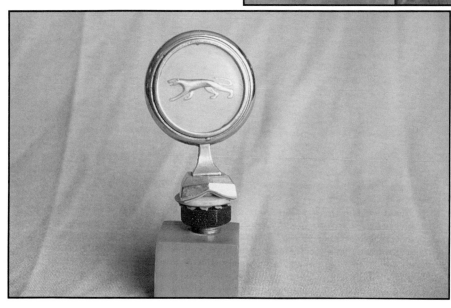

**YEAR:** 1974
**MODEL:** Mercury
**INF:** Cougar
D4WB 8B 343AA

**#0074**

U. S. Hood Ornaments and More . . .

## MERCURY

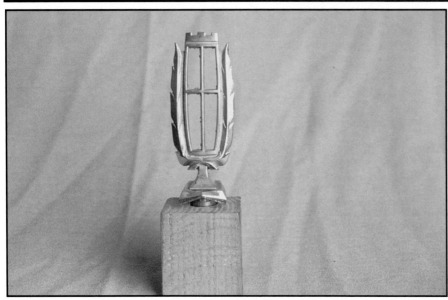

**YEAR:** 1976
**MODEL:** Mercury
**INF:** D5MB8 13343

#0076

**YEAR:** 1979
**MODEL:** Mercury
**INF:** D8KB 16850 AB

#0079

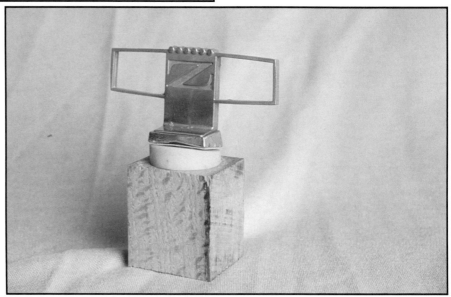

**YEAR:** 1980
**MODEL:** Mercury
**INF:** Grand Marquis
85021 10000595

#0080

*U. S. Hood Ornaments and More . . .*

# MERCURY

**MODEL:** Mercury
**INF:** Mercury script
8CO 46 AA

#0501

**MODEL:** Mercury
**INF:** Script Mercury

#0502

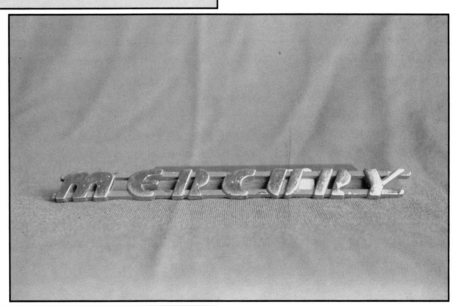

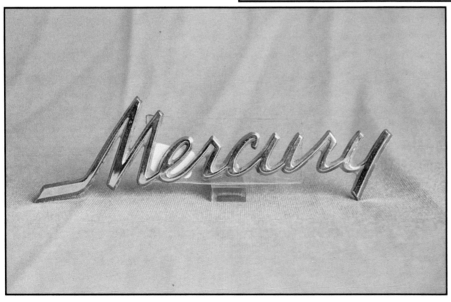

**MODEL:** Mercury
**INF:** C9MB 8B354 A
Script

#0503

U. S. Hood Ornaments and More . . .

# MERCURY

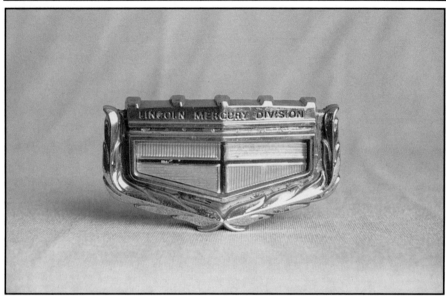

**MODEL:** Mercury
**INF:** D14B 16850 AB
1950-1951

#0504

**MODEL:** Mercury
**INF:** 3810011
Brougham

#0505

**MODEL:** Mercury
**INF:** C9MB 6557A
56A; 1969

#0506

*U. S. Hood Ornaments and More . . .*

## MERCURY

**MODEL:** Mercury
**INF:** Shield;
1949-1950

#0507

**MODEL:** Mercury
**INF:** Monterey
BG 16098-A 9700

#0508

U. S. Hood Ornaments and More . . .

# NASH

**YEAR:** 1936
**MODEL:** Nash
**INF:** 90757-2854

#0036

**YEAR:** 1935-1936
**MODEL:** Nash
**INF:** Lafayette 4088

#0136

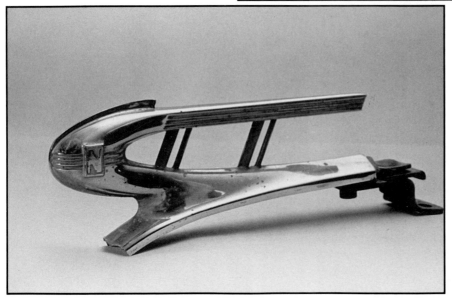

**YEAR:** 1938
**MODEL:** Nash
**INF:** 2925-3 Ambassador

#0038

U. S. Hood Ornaments and More . . .

# NASH

**YEAR:** 1946
**MODEL:** Nash
**INF:** 7" lady face center piece

**#0046**

**YEAR:** 1948
**MODEL:** Nash
**INF:** 521426
Winged lady

**#0048**

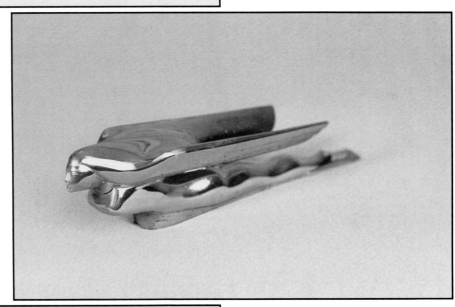

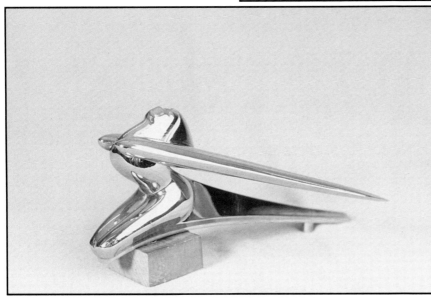

**YEAR:** 1952
**MODEL:** Nash
**INF:** 3114126
125407-1
Kneeling winged lady

**#0052**

*United States Hood Ornaments and More . . .*

# NASH

**YEAR:** 1953
**MODEL:** Nash
**INF:** 519948
25574-1
Flying lady

**#0053**

**YEAR:** 1953
**MODEL:** Nash
**INF:** Lady only

**#0153**

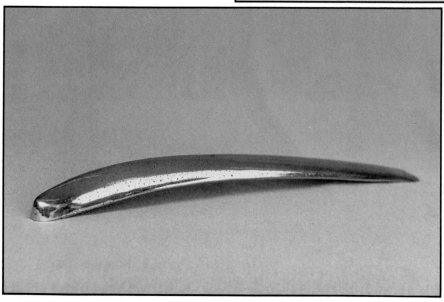

**YEAR:** 1955
**MODEL:** Nash
**INF:** 653 Rambler

**#0055**

*United States Hood Ornaments and More . . .*

## NASH

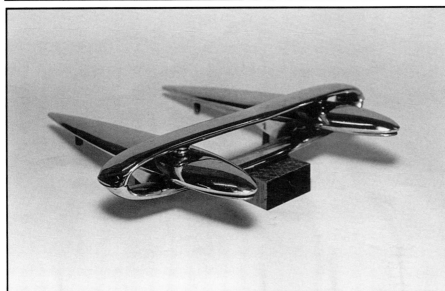

**YEAR:** 1956-1957
**MODEL:** Nash
**INF:** Stamped steel with two pods

#0056

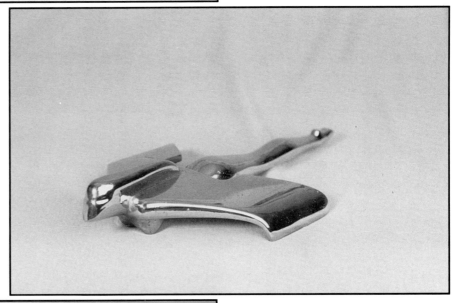

**YEAR:** 1957
**MODEL:** Nash
**INF:** 25218-1
Broad curved flying lady

#0057

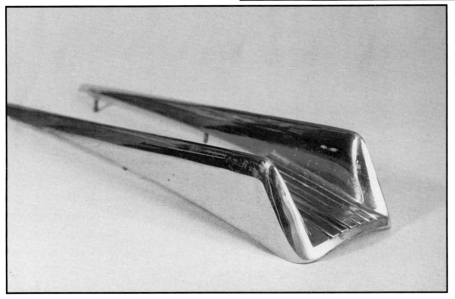

**YEAR:** 1957
**MODEL:** Nash
**INF:** Rambler
3151363

#0157

U. S. Hood Ornaments and More . . .

# NASH

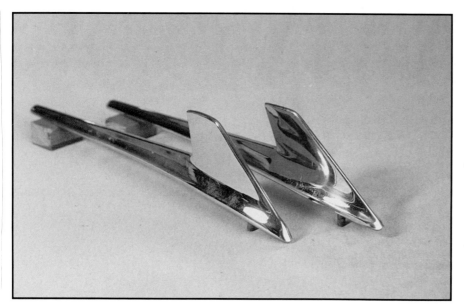

**YEAR:** 1959
**MODEL:** Nash
**INF:** Rambler 13421953; one pair fender emblems

#0059

**MODEL:** Nash
**INF:** 3554054
290 Rambler

#0601

## OLDSMOBILE

**YEAR:** 1932
**MODEL:** Olds
**INF:** 85304
Bird

#0032

**YEAR:** 1933
**MODEL:** Olds
**INF:** Bird base; 8 cylinder

#0033

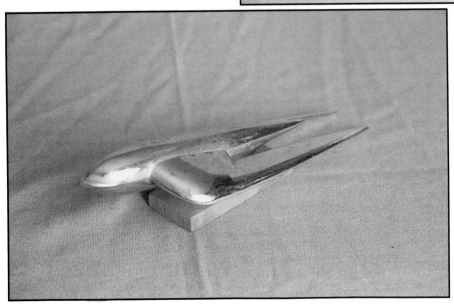

**YEAR:** 1933
**MODEL:** Olds
**INF:** 6 cylinder

#0133

U. S. Hood Ornaments and More . . .

# OLDSMOBILE

**YEAR:** 1934
**MODEL:** Olds
**INF:** 90776
Goddess

**#0034**

**YEAR:** 1935
**MODEL:** Olds
**INF:** PT-T-29729

**#0035**

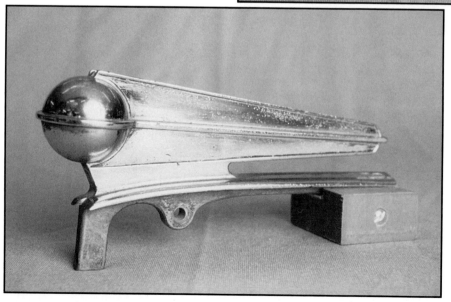

**YEAR:** 1935
**MODEL:** Olds
**INF:** 8 cylinder

**#0135**

U. S. Hood Ornaments and More . . .

## OLDSMOBILE

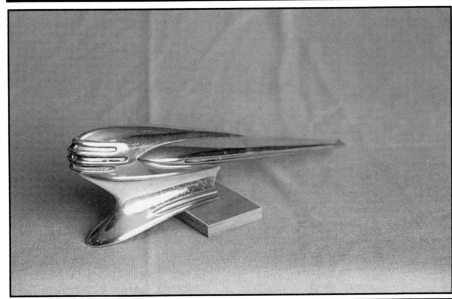

**YEAR:** 1936
**MODEL:** Olds
**INF:** No number; broken base

**#0036**

**YEAR:** 1938
**MODEL:** Olds
**INF:** T-29767

**#0038**

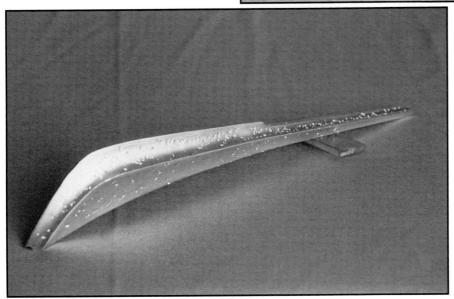

**YEAR:** 1939
**MODEL:** Olds
**INF:** 711312

**#0039**

U. S. Hood Ornaments and More . . .

## OLDSMOBILE

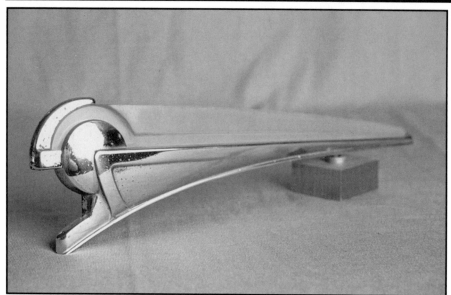

**YEAR:** 1940
**MODEL:** Olds
**INF:** 413420
8 cylinder

**#0040**

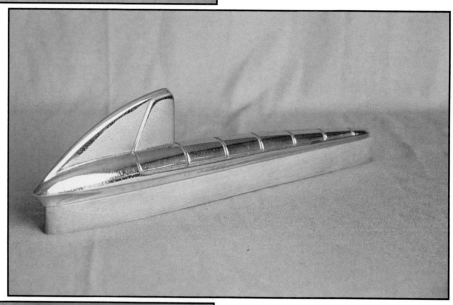

**YEAR:** 1941
**MODEL:** Olds
**INF:** 414585

**#0041**

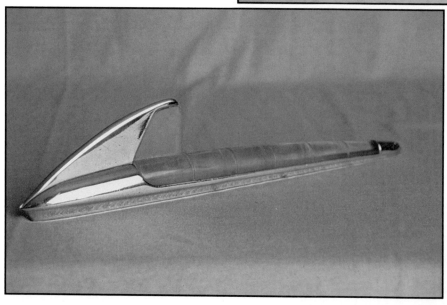

**YEAR:** 1941
**MODEL:** Olds
**INF:** 414578

**#0141**

U. S. Hood Ornaments and More . . .

## OLDSMOBILE

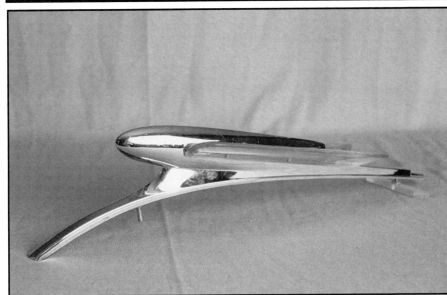

**YEAR:** 1946-1947
**MODEL:** Olds
**INF:** 410873
Clear lucite turned-up wings; Deluxe

**#0046**

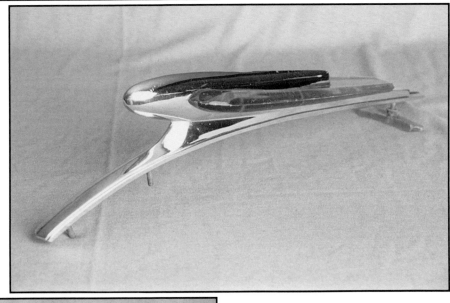

**YEAR:** 1946-1947
**MODEL:** Olds
**INF:** 418733
Red lucite flat wing design; Deluxe

**#0047**

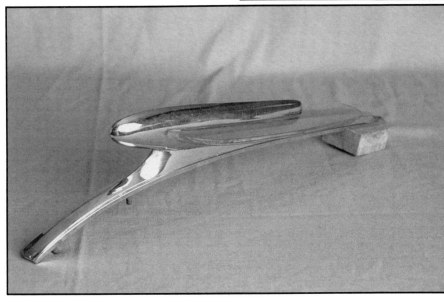

**YEAR:** 1946-1947
**MODEL:** Olds
**INF:** 418733
Replacement flat wing

**#0147**

U. S. Hood Ornaments and More . . .

## OLDSMOBILE

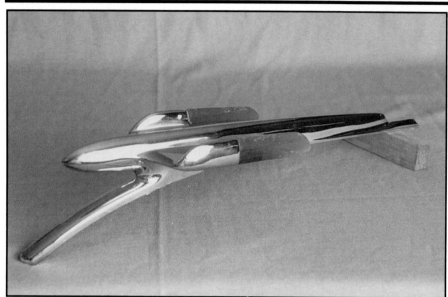

**YEAR:** 1948
**MODEL:** Olds
**INF:** 555088
555089
Red plastic wings

**#0048**

**YEAR:** 1949
**MODEL:** Olds
**INF:** 557740

**#0049**

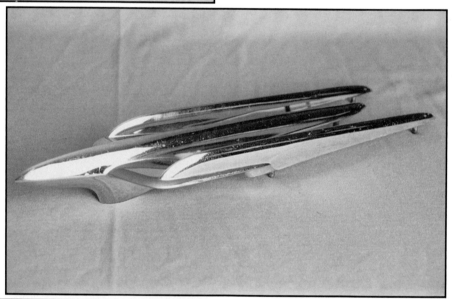

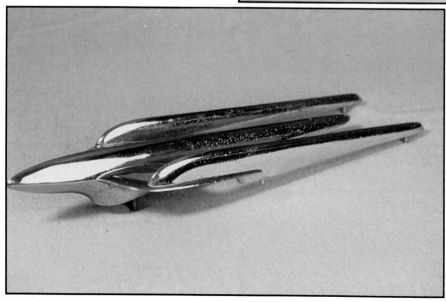

**YEAR:** 1949
**MODEL:** Olds
**INF:** 555998
Center shaft

**#0149**

U. S. Hood Ornaments and More . . .

## OLDSMOBILE

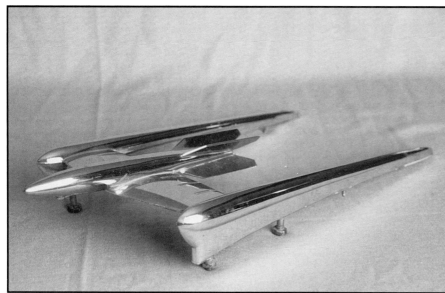

**YEAR:** 1950
**MODEL:** Olds
**INF:** 658860

**#0050**

**YEAR:** 1950
**MODEL:** Olds
**INF:** AC-1550167

**#0150**

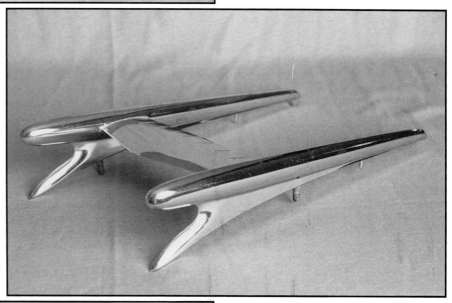

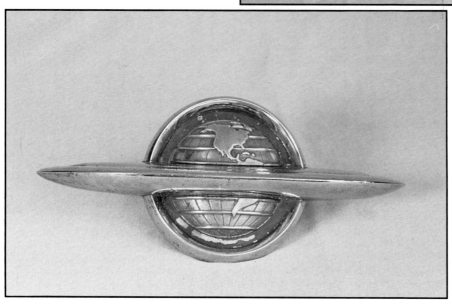

**YEAR:** 1950
**MODEL:** Olds
**INF:** 560058
World

**#0250**

U. S. Hood Ornaments and More . . .

## OLDSMOBILE

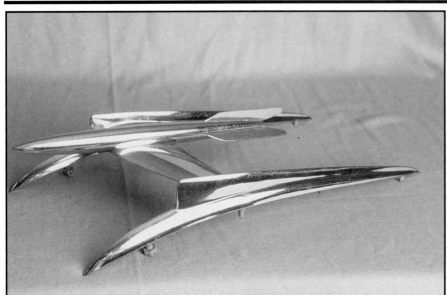

**YEAR:** 1951
**MODEL:** Olds
**INF:** 561063
561084

**#0051**

**YEAR:** 1952
**MODEL:** Olds
**INF:** 561681

**#0052**

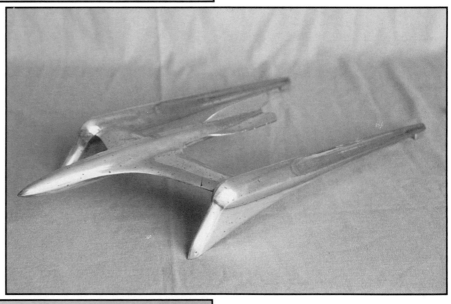

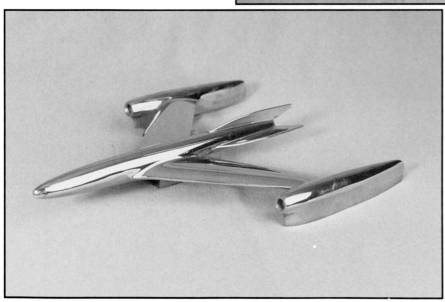

**YEAR:** 1953-1954
**MODEL:** Olds
**INF:** 564578
T29703

**#0053**

## OLDSMOBILE

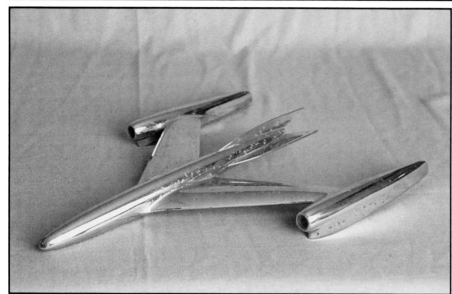

**YEAR:** 1954
**MODEL:** Olds
**INF:** 563715

**#0054**

**YEAR:** 1955
**MODEL:** Olds
**INF:** 566355

**#0055**

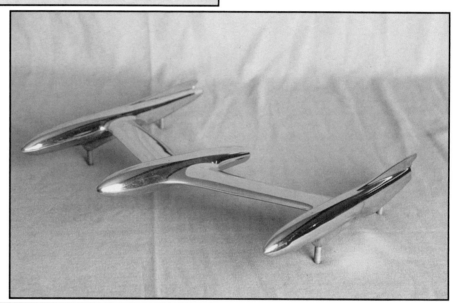

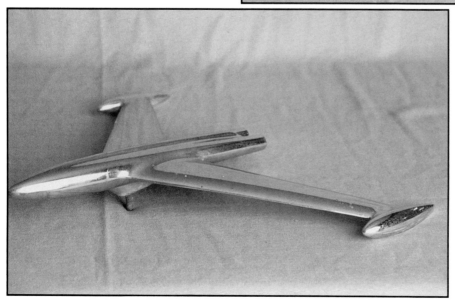

**YEAR:** 1956
**MODEL:** Olds
**INF:** 567532

**#0056**

## OLDSMOBILE

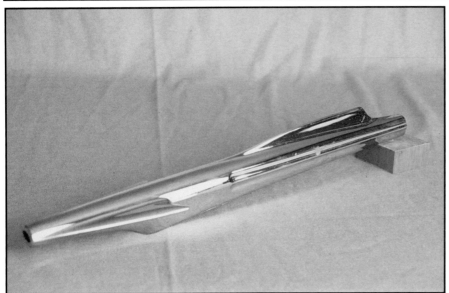

**YEAR:** 1956
**MODEL:** Olds
**INF:** 572272
13544

#0156

**YEAR:** 1956-1957
**MODEL:** Olds
**INF:** 569222
26706

#0256

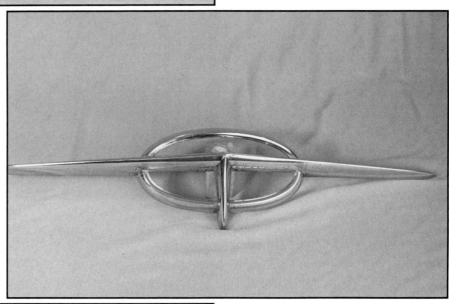

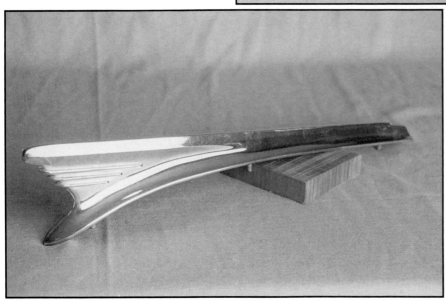

**YEAR:** 1957
**MODEL:** Olds
**INF:** 571056 -
11302

#0057

## OLDSMOBILE

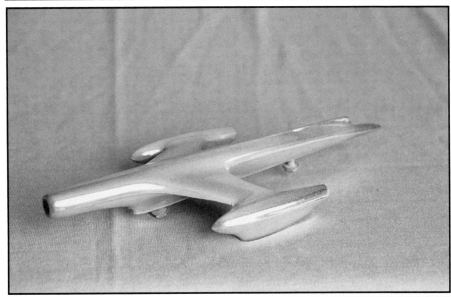

**YEAR:** 1957
**MODEL:** Olds
**INF:** 570460
RH fender

**#0157**

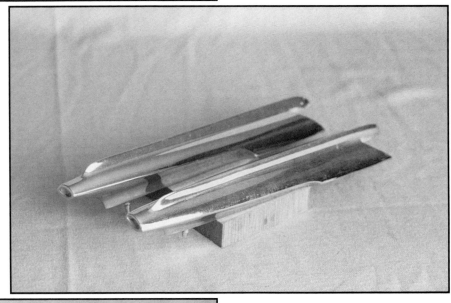

**YEAR:** 1959
**MODEL:** Olds
**INF:** 575599 LH
575598 RH
Fender

**#0059**

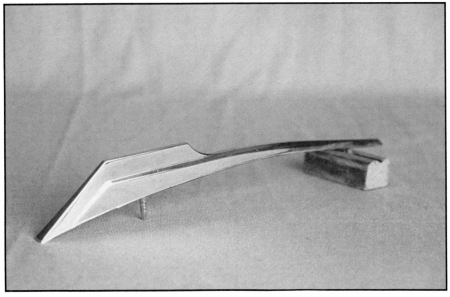

**YEAR:** 1966
**MODEL:** Olds
**INF:** 3887580 F85

**#0066**

U. S. Hood Ornaments and More . . .

## OLDSMOBILE

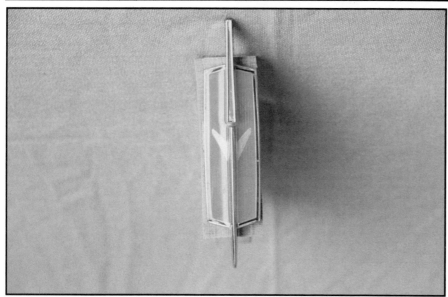

**YEAR:** 1973
**MODEL:** Olds
**INF:** Cutlass
413522 12504

**#0073**

**YEAR:** 1977
**MODEL:** Olds
**INF:** 551536
Cutlass

**#0077**

**YEAR:** 1981
**MODEL:** Olds
**INF:** 562206 92150
Diesel

**#0081**

## OLDSMOBILE

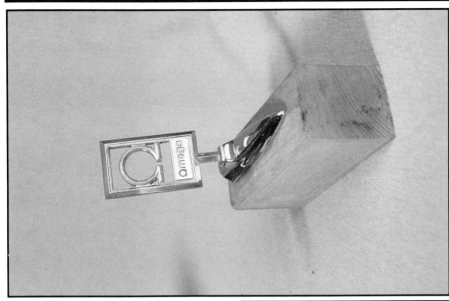

**YEAR:** 1981
**MODEL:** Olds
**INF:** 562180
Omega

**#0181**

**MODEL:** Olds
**INF:** Cutlass script

**#0601**

**MODEL:** Olds
**INF:** Toronado script

**#0602**

*U. S. Hood Ornaments and More . . .*

# OLDSMOBILE

**MODEL:** Olds
**INF:** 9858568
Olds script

#0603

**MODEL:** Olds
**INF:** Ninety Eight script

#0604

U. S. Hood Ornaments and More . . .

# OLDSMOBILE

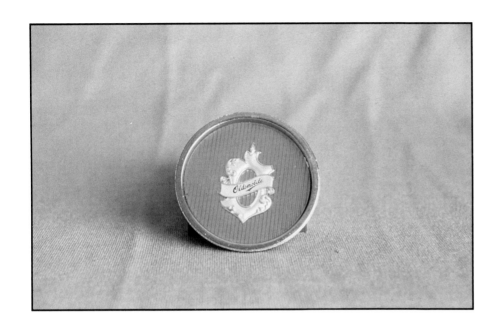

**MODEL:** Olds
**INF:** Center
254842

**#0605**

**MODEL:** Olds
**INF:** Emblem

**#0606**

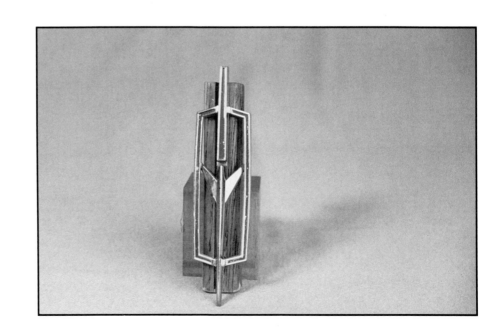

## PACKARD

**YEAR:** 1937-38
**MODEL:** Packard
**INF:** Deluxe Goddess of Speed

#0037

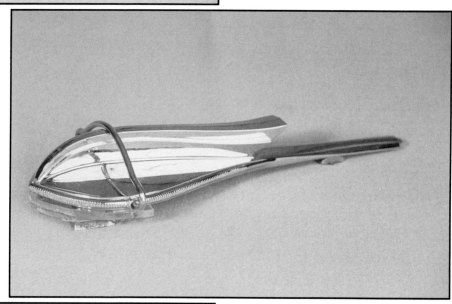

**YEAR:** 1938
**MODEL:** Packard
**INF:** 342900

#0039

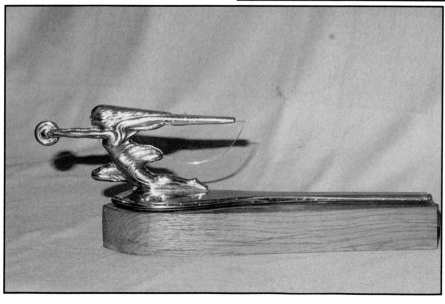

**YEAR:** 1939
**MODEL:** Packard
**INF:** 114358
Flying lady

#0040

U. S. Hood Ornaments and More . . .

## PACKARD

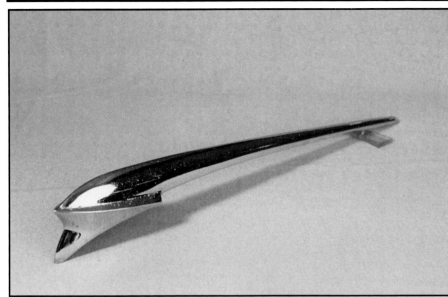

**YEAR:** 1946
**MODEL:** Packard
**INF:** 383544 7086
20" long

**#0046**

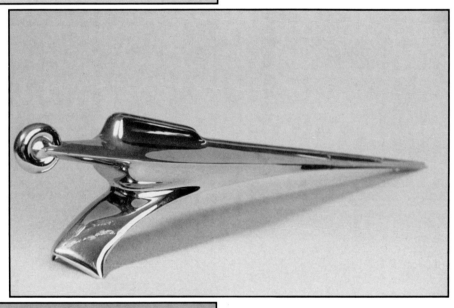

**YEAR:** 1946-1947
**MODEL:** Packard
**INF:** 383818
21" long

**#0047**

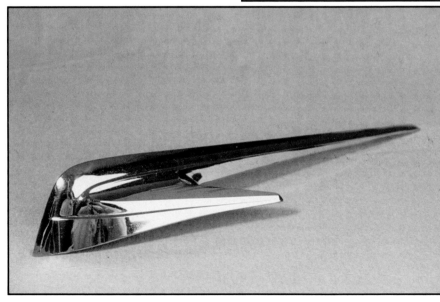

**YEAR:** 1948-1950
**MODEL:** Packard
**INF:** 394755 7577
18" long; 6-1/4" wide

**#0048**

# PACKARD

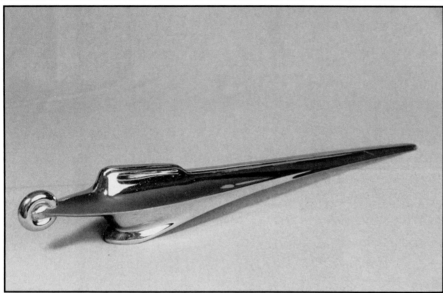

**YEAR:** 1948-1951
**MODEL:** Packard
**INF:** 394756
21-1/2" long

**#0049**

**YEAR:** 1948-1951
**MODEL:** Packard
**INF:** 151310

**#0051**

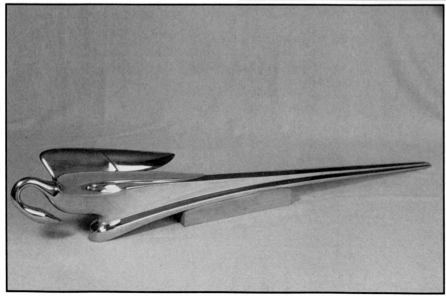

**YEAR:** 1952
**MODEL:** Packard
**INF:** 444874
CB22052
28" long' 4" wide

**#0052**

U. S. Hood Ornaments and More . . .

# PACKARD

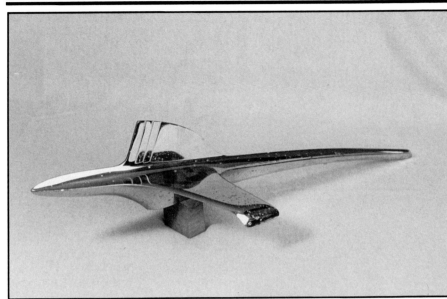

**YEAR:** 1951-1953
**MODEL:** Packard
**INF:** 422445
22-1/2" long;  9" wing span

**#0053**

**YEAR:** 1953
**MODEL:** Packard
**INF:** Ship wheel

**#0153**

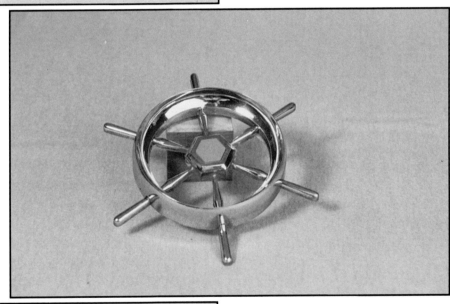

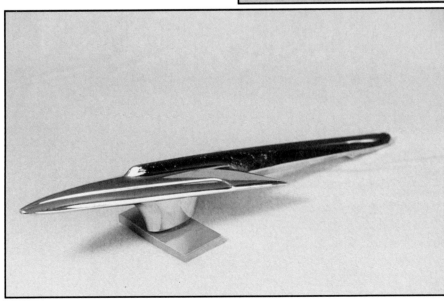

**YEAR:** 1954
**MODEL:** Packard
**INF:** 448798 Clipper
17-1/2" long;  4" wing span

**#0154**

U. S. Hood Ornaments and More . . .

## PACKARD

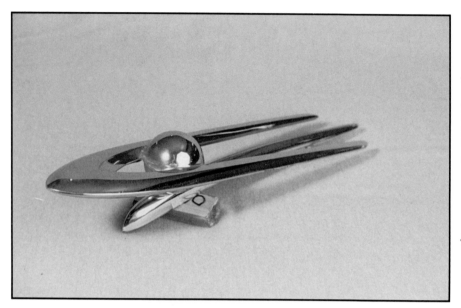

**YEAR:** 1955
**MODEL:** Packard
**INF:** 466446  466448
15" long; 3-1/2" wide

#0055

**YEAR:** 1956
**MODEL:** Packard
**INF:** 6478502
18" long; 6" wing span

#0056

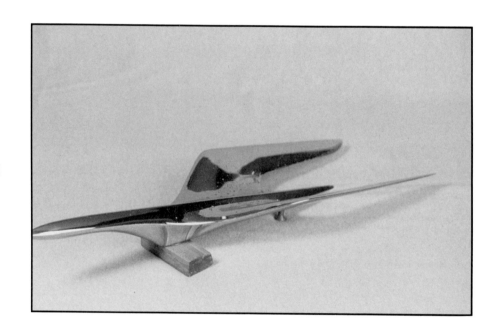

U. S. Hood Ornaments and More . . .

# PACKARD

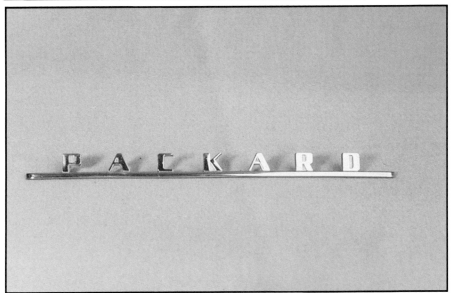

**MODEL:** Packard
**INF:** 415670 8293
Packard script

#0011

**MODEL:** Packard
**INF:** 4665-42
Clipper script

#0012

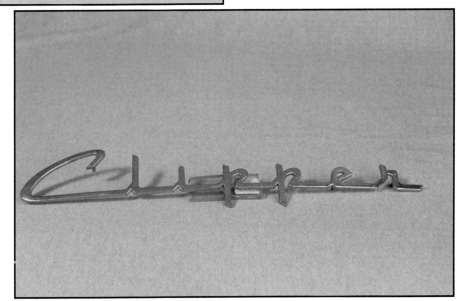

**YEAR:** 1950
**MODEL:** Packard
**INF:** Grill emblem

#0013

U. S. Hood Ornaments and More . . .

# PLYMOUTH

**YEAR:** 1931-1932
**MODEL:** Plymouth
**INF:** Pat. 86521
Goddess cap

**#0031**

**YEAR:** 1931
**MODEL:** Plymouth
**INF:** PC Cooper;
broken

**#0131**

**YEAR:** 1934-1935
**MODEL:** Plymouth
**INF:** 645091
Broken front sail

**#0035**

U. S. Hood Ornaments and More . . .

## PLYMOUTH

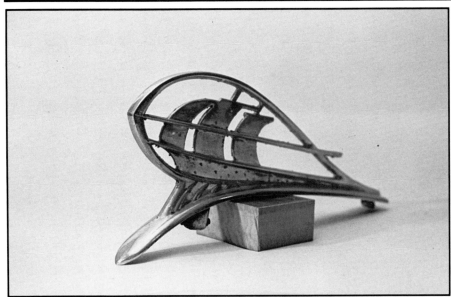

**YEAR:** 1936
**MODEL:** Plymouth
**INF:** 653596

#0036

**YEAR:** 1936
**MODEL:** Plymouth
**INF:** 655499 P1 P2

#0136

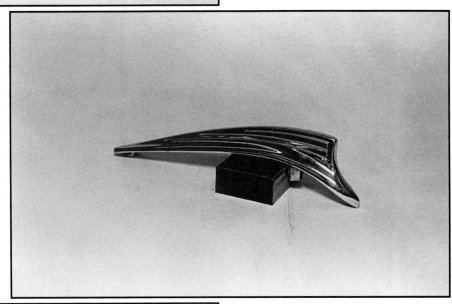

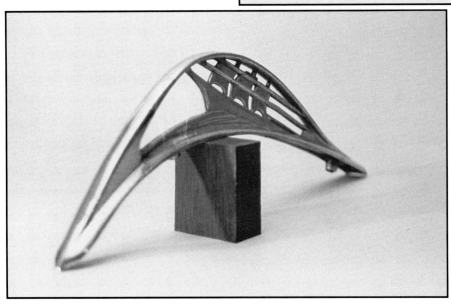

**YEAR:** 1937
**MODEL:** Plymouth
**INF:** 741919

#0037

U. S. Hood Ornaments and More . . .

## PLYMOUTH

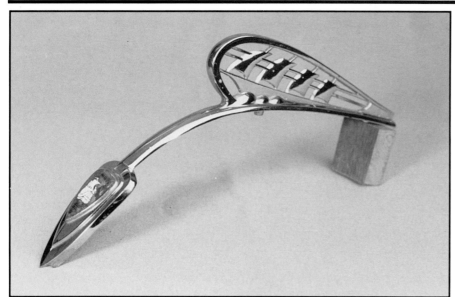

**YEAR:** 1938
**MODEL:** Plymouth
**INF:** 368791

**#0038**

**YEAR:** 1939
**MODEL:** Plymouth
**INF:** 591297 3926A

**#0039**

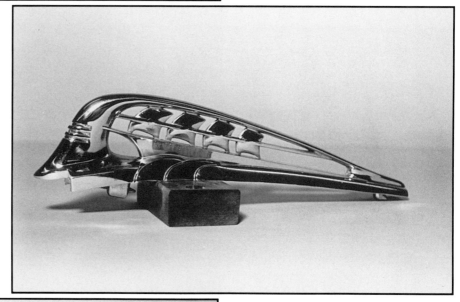

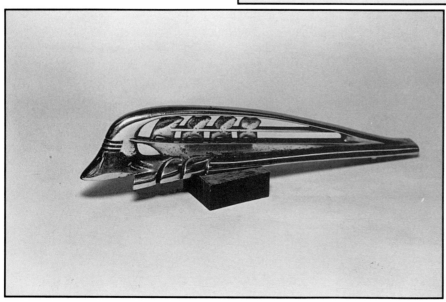

**YEAR:** 1939
**MODEL:** Plymouth
**INF:** 793389

**#0139**

U. S. Hood Ornaments and More . . . .

## PLYMOUTH

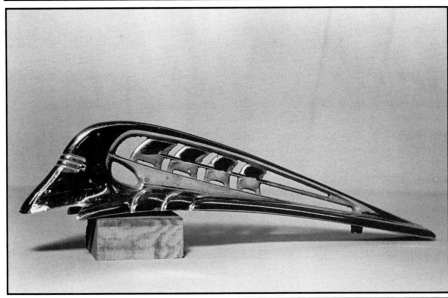

**YEAR:** 1940
**MODEL:** Plymouth
**INF:** 847904

**#0040**

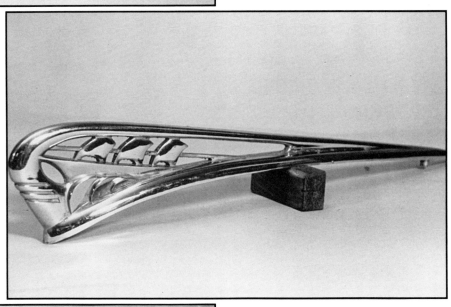

**YEAR:** 1941
**MODEL:** Plymouth
**INF:** 901955

**#0041**

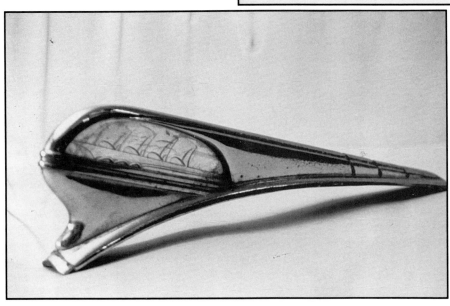

**YEAR:** 1942
**MODEL:** Plymouth
**INF:** 972205

**#0042**

U. S. Hood Ornaments and More . . .

# PLYMOUTH

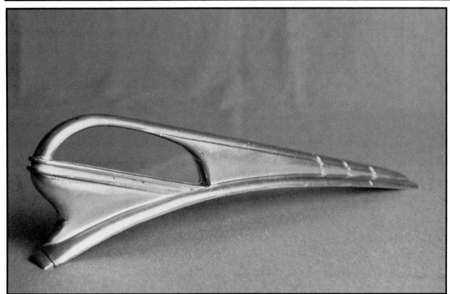

**YEAR:** 1942
**MODEL:** Plymouth
**INF:** Lead style

**#0142**

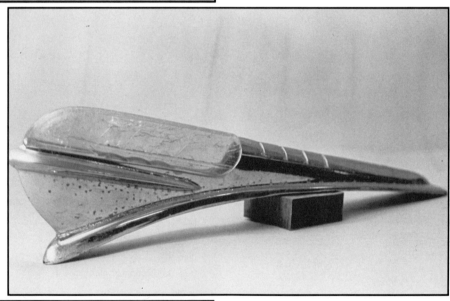

**YEAR:** 1946-1948
**MODEL:** Plymouth
**INF:** 1065766

**#0046**

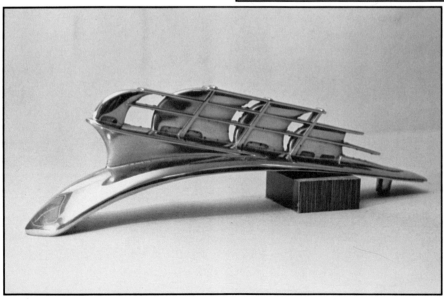

**YEAR:** 1949
**MODEL:** Plymouth
**INF:** 1298931 BB

**#0049**

U. S. Hood Ornaments and More . . .

## PLYMOUTH

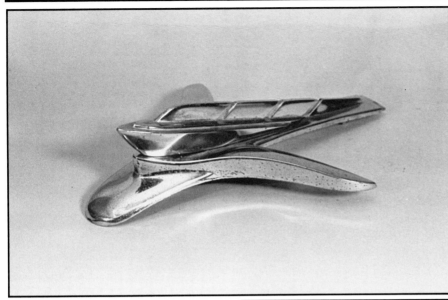

**YEAR:** 1950
**MODEL:** Plymouth
**INF:** 1373394

**#0050**

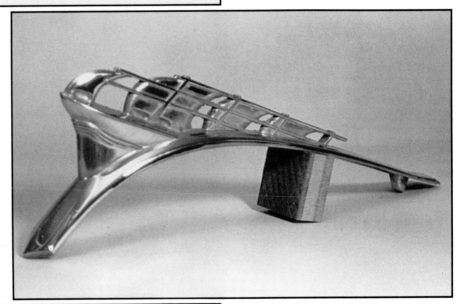

**YEAR:** 1950
**MODEL:** Plymouth
**INF:** 1335472

**#0150**

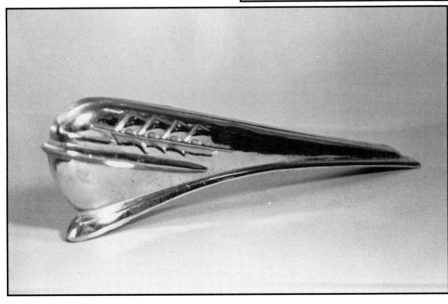

**YEAR:** 1952
**MODEL:** Plymouth
**INF:** No number

**#0052**

U. S. Hood Ornaments and More . . .

# PLYMOUTH

**YEAR:** 1952
**MODEL:** Plymouth
**INF:** 1456285
Emblem

**#0152**

**YEAR:** 1953
**MODEL:** Plymouth
**INF:** 1456363

**#0053**

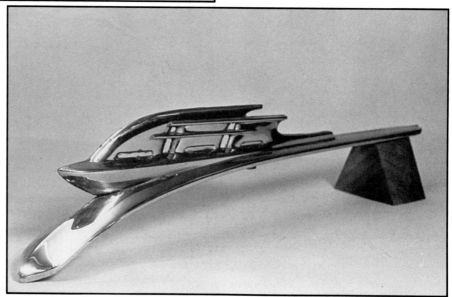

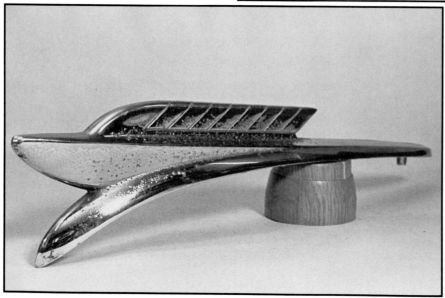

**YEAR:** 1954
**MODEL:** Plymouth
**INF:** 1494713

**#0054**

U. S. Hood Ornaments and More . . .

# PLYMOUTH

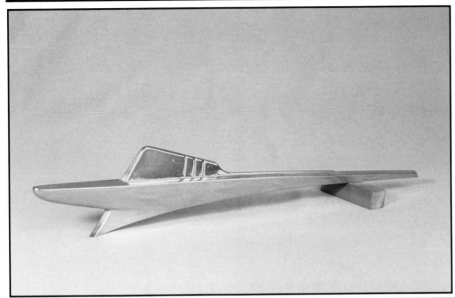

**YEAR:** 1955
**MODEL:** Plymouth
**INF:** 1599468

#0055

**YEAR:** 1963
**MODEL:** Plymouth
**INF:** 2276331
Red & blue in circle

#0063

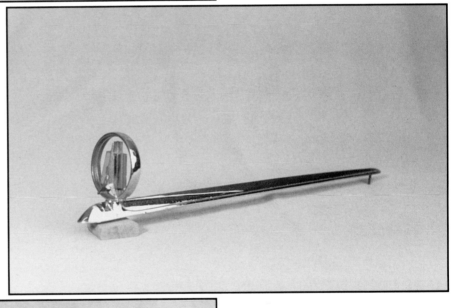

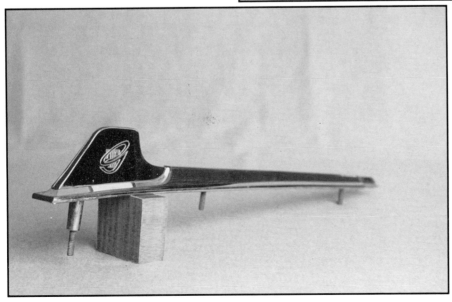

**YEAR:** 1965
**MODEL:** Plymouth
**INF:** 2449727
Red-white-blue
2524049  254441

#0065

U. S. Hood Ornaments and More . . .

## PLYMOUTH

**YEAR:** 1978
**MODEL:** Plymouth
**INF:** Hood ornament

#0078

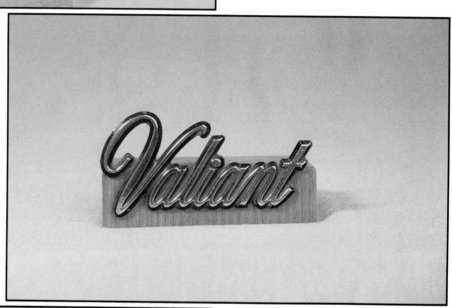

**MODEL:** Plymouth
**INF:** 3811 435
31025 3
Valiant script

#0801

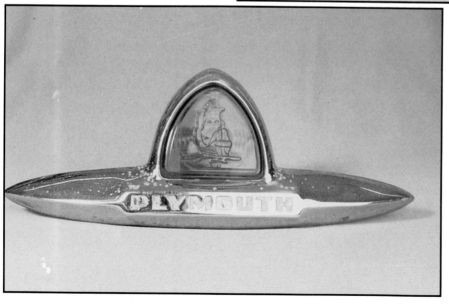

**MODEL:** Plymouth
**INF:** 1148894
CB13539

#0802

## PLYMOUTH

**MODEL:** Plymouth
**INF:** Plymouth emblem

#0803

**MODEL:** Plymouth
**INF:** Eight shield

#0804

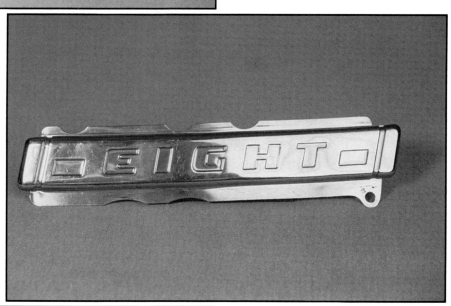

**MODEL:** Plymouth
**INF:** 1149072
Emblem

#0805

U. S. Hood Ornaments and More . . .

# PONTIAC

**YEAR:** 1932
**MODEL:** Pontiac
**INF:** Pat. 87231
Indian head in circle

#0032

**YEAR:** 1936
**MODEL:** Pontiac
**INF:** 98069
Indian in oval

#0036

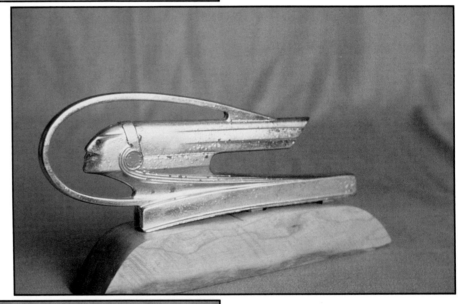

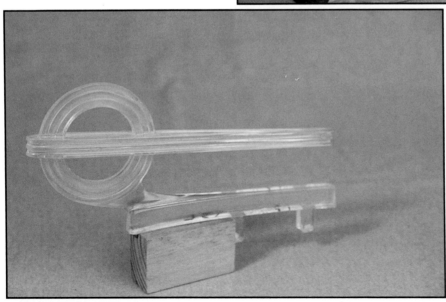

**YEAR:** 1936
**MODEL:** Pontiac
**INF:** 8 cylinder

#0136

U. S. Hood Ornaments and More . . .

## PONTIAC

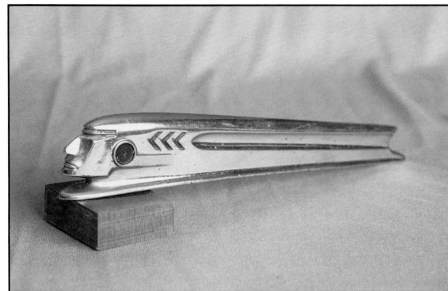

**YEAR:** 1937
**MODEL:** Pontiac
**INF:** 29757-701998

**#0037**

**YEAR:** 1938
**MODEL:** Pontiac
**INF:** 29771

**#0038**

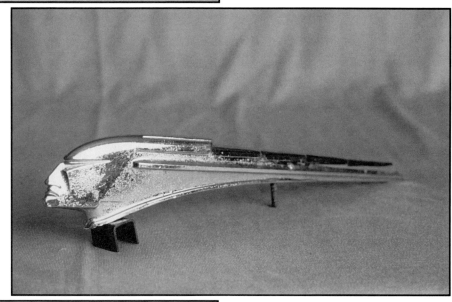

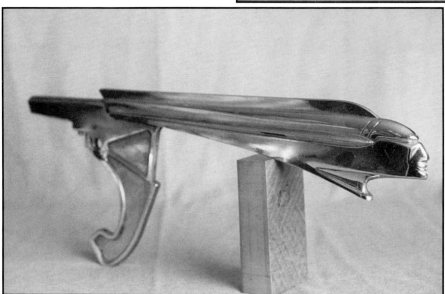

**YEAR:** 1939-1940
**MODEL:** Pontiac
**INF:** 729795

**#0039**

## PONTIAC

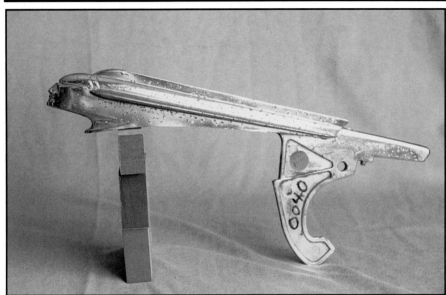

**YEAR:** 1940
**MODEL:** Pontiac
**INF:** 29795
Latch type

**#0040**

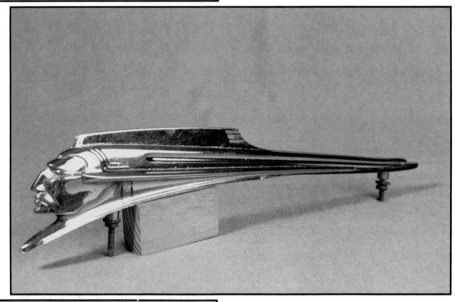

**YEAR:** 1941
**MODEL:** Pontiac
**INF:** T29814
14" long

**#0041**

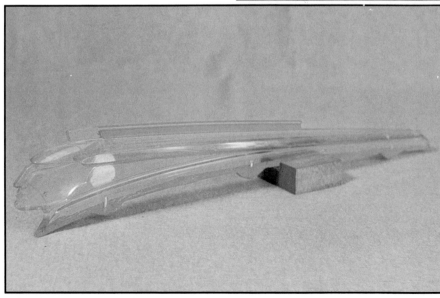

**YEAR:** 1942
**MODEL:** Pontiac
**INF:** 519948 519947
Clear insert; 15-1/2" long

**#0042**

*U. S. Hood Ornaments and More . . .*

## PONTIAC

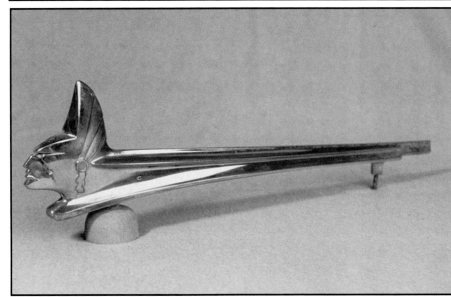

**YEAR:** 1946
**MODEL:** Pontiac
**INF:** 508614
16-1/2" long

**#0046**

**YEAR:** 1946
**MODEL:** Pontiac
**INF:** 508615
With red insert;
18" long

**#0246**

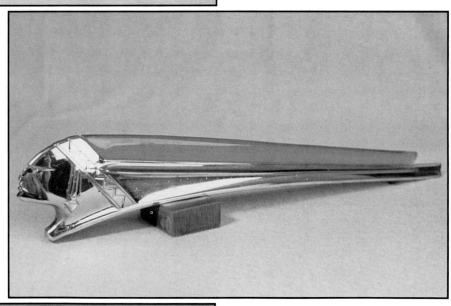

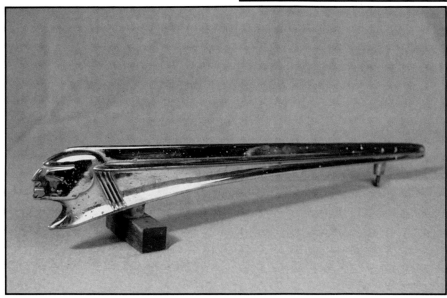

**YEAR:** 1947
**MODEL:** Pontiac
**INF:** 509591

**#0047**

U. S. Hood Ornaments and More . . .

## PONTIAC

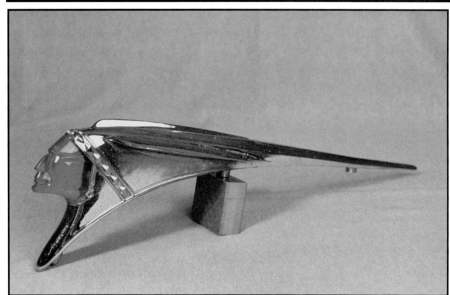

**YEAR:** 1948
**MODEL:** Pontiac
**INF:** 512714
17" long

**#0048**

**YEAR:** 1949
**MODEL:** Pontiac
**INF:** 510565
Red wing; chrome face;
19" long

**#0049**

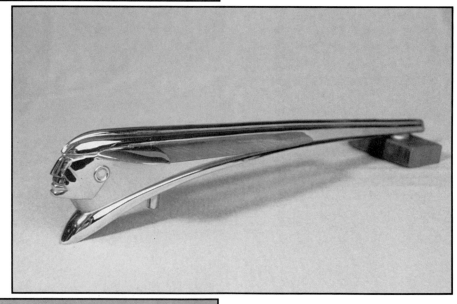

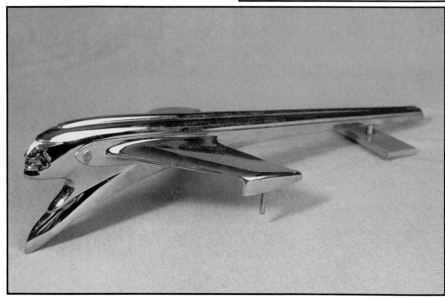

**YEAR:** 1950
**MODEL:** Pontiac
**INF:** 513747
Chrome face; 20"
long; 7" wide

**#0050**

U. S. Hood Ornaments and More . . .

## PONTIAC

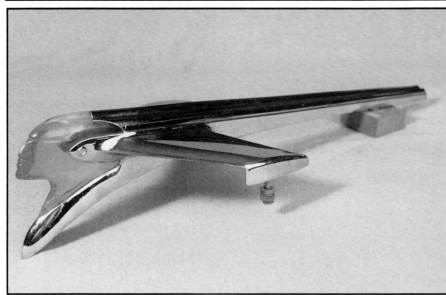

**YEAR:** 1950
**MODEL:** Pontiac
**INF:** 513872  513870
Amber insert;
19-1/2" long; 7" wide

**#0250**

**YEAR:** 1951
**MODEL:** Pontiac
**INF:** 515594

**#0051**

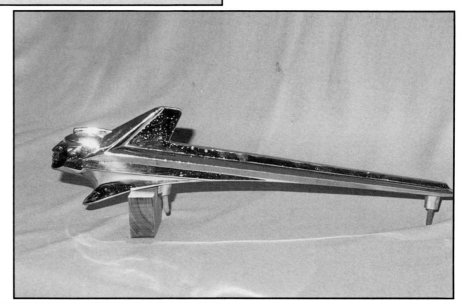

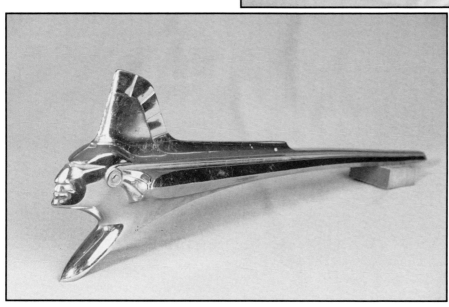

**YEAR:** 1951-1952
**MODEL:** Pontiac
**INF:** 514855
Production type;
18-1/2" long

**#0251**

*U. S. Hood Ornaments and More . . .*

## PONTIAC

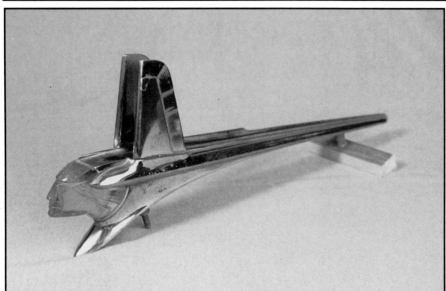

**YEAR:** 1953
**MODEL:** Pontiac
**INF:** 516830
19" long

**#0053**

**YEAR:** 1953
**MODEL:** Pontiac
**INF:** 516780
16-1/2" long

**#0253**

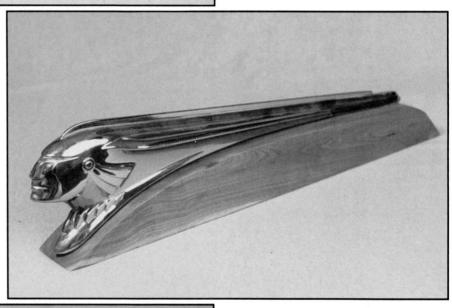

**YEAR:** 1954
**MODEL:** Pontiac
**INF:** 517629
Production model;
15" long; 8" wide

**#0054**

U. S. Hood Ornaments and More . . .

# PONTIAC

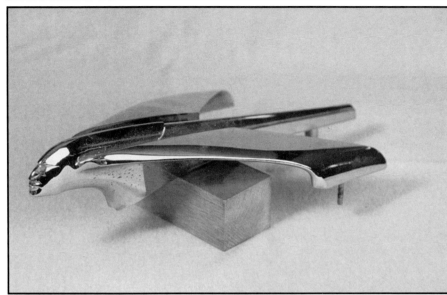

**YEAR:** 1953-1954
**MODEL:** Pontiac
**INF:** 517658
17" long; 8" wide

#0154

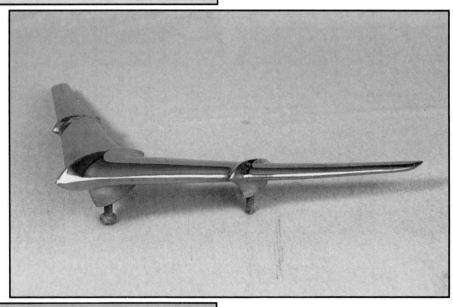

**YEAR:** 1955
**MODEL:** Pontiac
**INF:** 519309
15" wing span

#0055

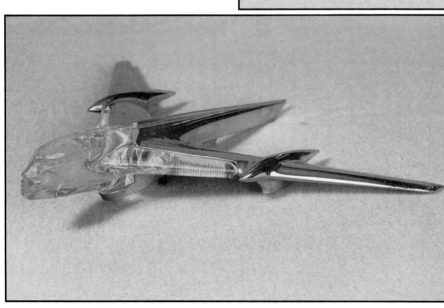

**YEAR:** 1955
**MODEL:** Pontiac
**INF:** Amber; all plastic; 14-1/2" wing span

#0155

U. S. Hood Ornaments and More . . .

## PONTIAC

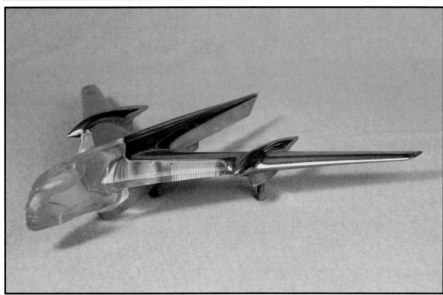

**YEAR:** 1955
**MODEL:** Pontiac
**INF:** 519948
Clear plastic;
14-1/2" wing span

#0255

**YEAR:** 1956
**MODEL:** Pontiac
**INF:** 523906
One pair lighted
fender units;
17" long

#0056

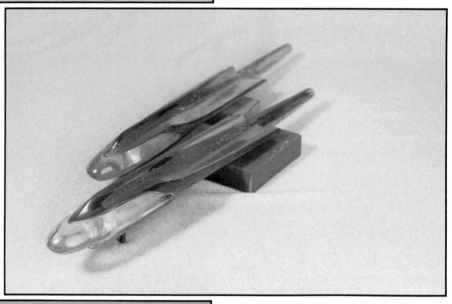

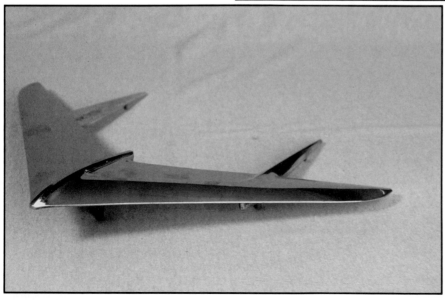

**YEAR:** 1956
**MODEL:** Pontiac
**INF:** 521426
Chieftain;
16" wing span

#0156

## PONTIAC

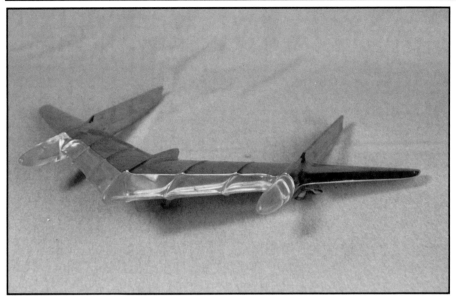

**YEAR:** 1957
**MODEL:** Pontiac
**INF:** 522077
Lighted emblem;
16" wing span

**#0057**

**YEAR:** 1957
**MODEL:** Pontiac
**INF:** 575381-
575380 L & R
675598-575599;
14" long

**#0257**

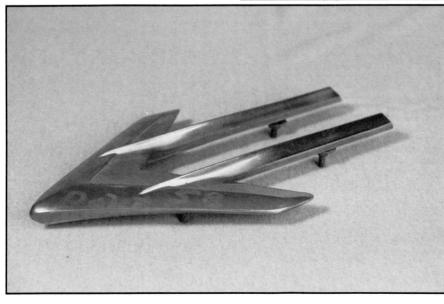

**YEAR:** 1958
**MODEL:** Pontiac
**INF:** 52927
RH fender; 11" long

**#0158**

U. S. Hood Ornaments and More . . .

## PONTIAC

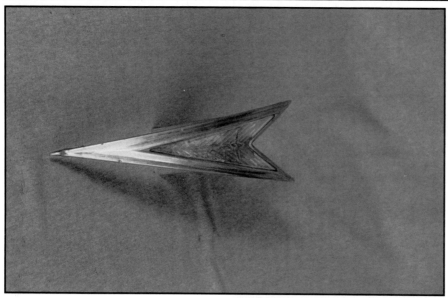

**YEAR:** 1959
**MODEL:** Pontiac
**INF:** Stamp V

#0159

**YEAR:** 1960
**MODEL:** Pontiac
**INF:** 10018466
10023376
Late '60 sunburst

#0069

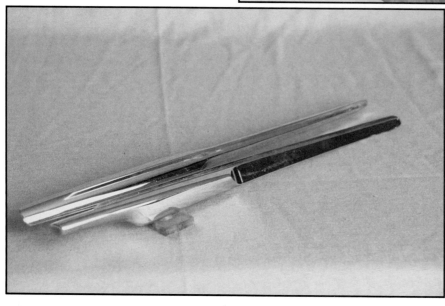

**YEAR:** 1962
**MODEL:** Pontiac
**INF:** 541254 LH
541255 LH
15" long

#0062

U. S. Hood Ornaments and More . . .

## PONTIAC

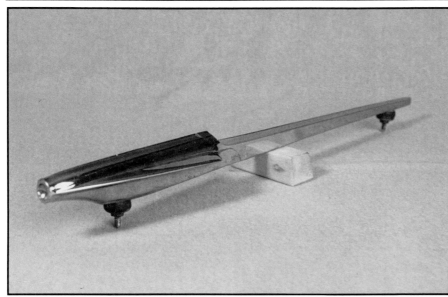

**YEAR:** 1965
**MODEL:** Pontiac
**INF:** 532850
17-1/2" long

**#0065**

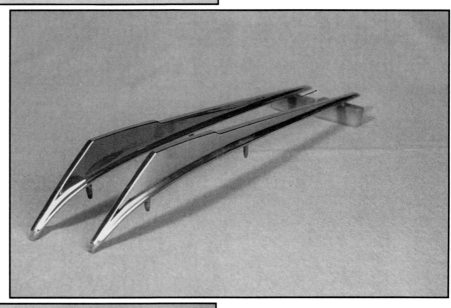

**YEAR:** 1965
**MODEL:** Pontiac
**INF:** 977402
17-1/2" long

**#0165**

**YEAR:** 1970
**MODEL:** Pontiac
**INF:** 10013754
10030137
Grand Prix

**#0070**

*U. S. Hood Ornaments and More . . .*

## PONTIAC

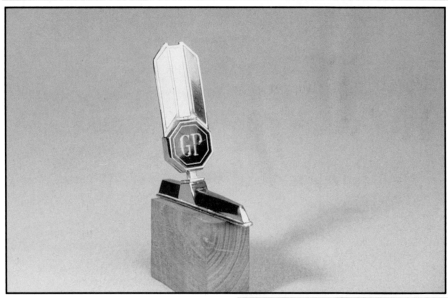

**YEAR:** 1970
**MODEL:** Pontiac
**INF:** 13393
Grand Prix

**#0170**

**MODEL:** Pontiac
**INF:** 77401
492009
Side name plate

**#0901**

**MODEL:** Pontiac
**INF:** Side emblem

**#0902**

*U. S. Hood Ornaments and More . . .*

# PONTIAC

**MODEL:** Pontiac
**INF:** Script

**#0903**

**MODEL:** Pontiac
**INF:**

**#0904**

*U. S. Hood Ornaments and More . . .*

# ROLLS ROYCE

The title of this book is U.S. Hood Ornaments and More. This is a More piece that was sent to me by Bob Boyd of Chetopa, Kansas, so we can enjoy it together. It is a Rolls-Royce mascot which was a classic and should join the USA collection for our enjoyment.

**YEAR:** 1914
**MODEL:** Rolls Royce
**INF:** Compliments of Bob Boyd, Chetopa, KS

**#0014**

U. S. Hood Ornaments and More . . .

## STUDEBAKER

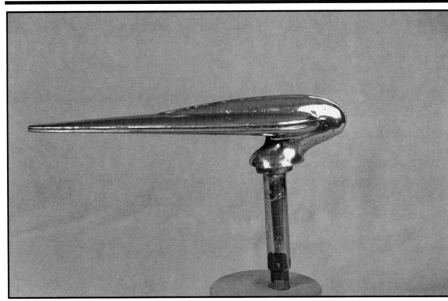

**YEAR:** 1937
**MODEL:** Studebaker
**INF:** Hood latch ornament

**#0037**

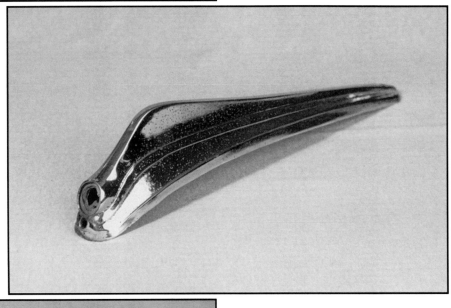

**YEAR:** 1938
**MODEL:** Studebaker
**INF:** 1528-F
Right hand with light

**#0038**

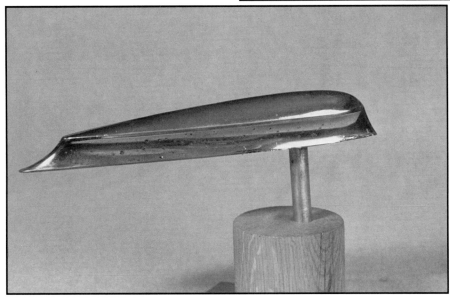

**YEAR:** 1938
**MODEL:** Studebaker
**INF:** 5051
Hood release

**#0138**

## STUDEBAKER

**YEAR:** 1941-1942
**MODEL:** Studebaker
**INF:** 5842
Glass insert assembly

#0041

**YEAR:** 1947
**MODEL:** Studebaker
**INF:** 7774
Long base; rocket;
Commander Land Cruiser

#0047

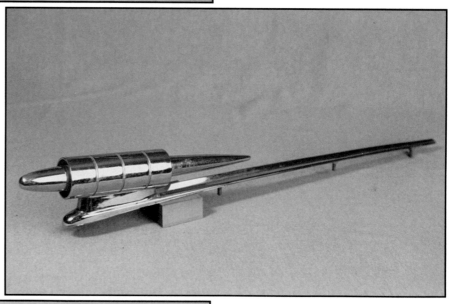

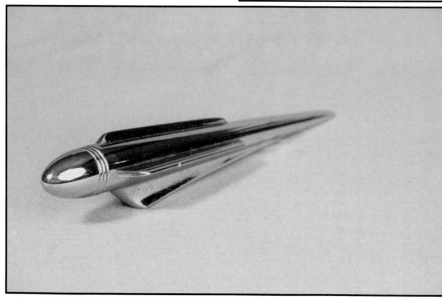

**YEAR:** 1948
**MODEL:** Studebaker
**INF:** 7718

#0048

U. S. Hood Ornaments and More . . .

## STUDEBAKER

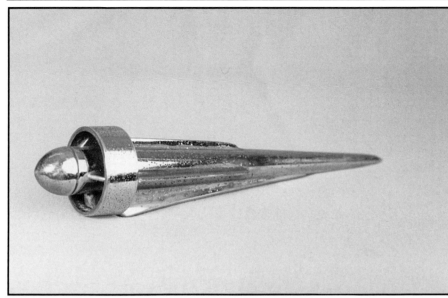

**YEAR:** 1949
**MODEL:** Studebaker
**INF:** X0-421

#0049

**YEAR:** 1950
**MODEL:** Studebaker
**INF:** 290406
Winged; clear plastic

#0050

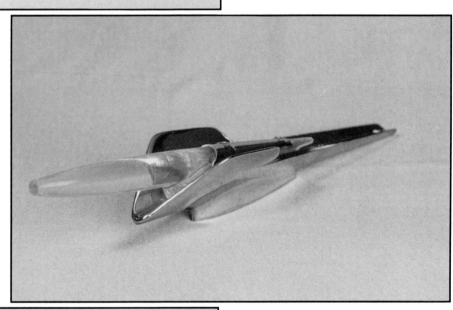

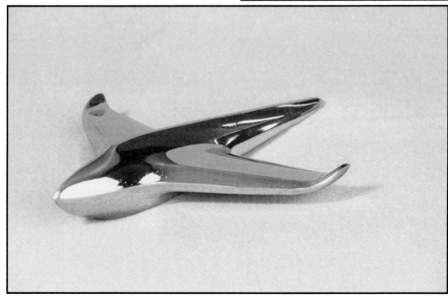

**YEAR:** 1951
**MODEL:** Studebaker
**INF:** 293270
Champion

#0051

U. S. Hood Ornaments and More . . .

## STUDEBAKER

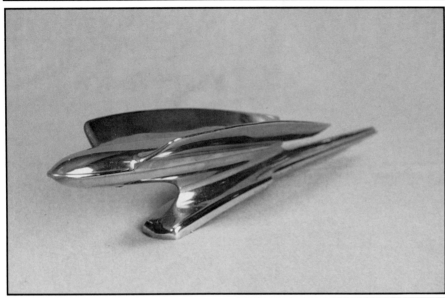

**YEAR:** 1952
**MODEL:** Studebaker
**INF:** X0-580
Stamped steel

**#0052**

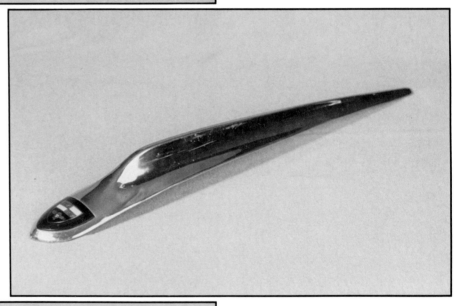

**YEAR:** 1953
**MODEL:** Studebaker
**INF:** 1630-28A   AC2318
14G  4H  Champion
Commander

**#0053**

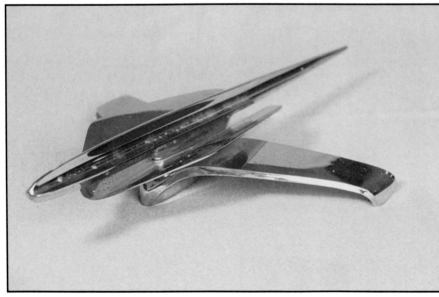

**YEAR:** 1954-1955
**MODEL:** Studebaker
**INF:** Commander
X0994  X0996

**#0054**

U. S. Hood Ornaments and More . . .

## STUDEBAKER

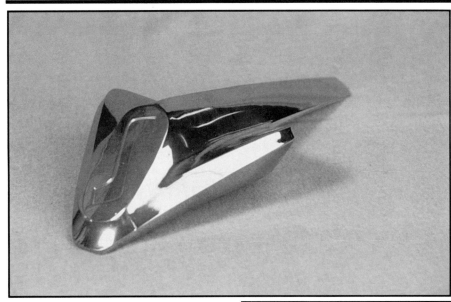

**YEAR:** 1955
**MODEL:** Studebaker
**INF:** Truck

**#0055**

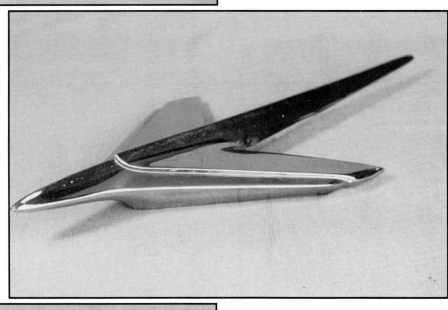

**YEAR:** 1955
**MODEL:** Studebaker
**INF:** 308691
Champion Roth

**#0155**

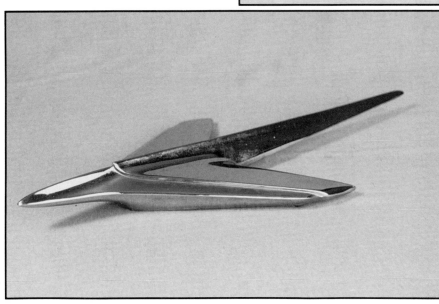

**YEAR:** 1955
**MODEL:** Studebaker
**INF:** 308961
Champion

**#0255**

U. S. Hood Ornaments and More . . .

# STUDEBAKER

**YEAR:** 1957
**MODEL:** Studebaker
**INF:** 1314741

#0057

**YEAR:** 1962-1963
**MODEL:** Studebaker
**INF:** 1342778-885B
1342775

#0062

U. S. Hood Ornaments and More . . .

## STUDEBAKER

**YEAR:** 1964-1966
**MODEL:** Studebaker
**INF:** 1358580
S emblem with name

#0064

**YEAR:** 1965
**MODEL:** Studebaker
**INF:** 1351226
Roth 942

#0065

U. S. Hood Ornaments and More . . .

# WHITE TRUCK

**YEAR:** 1959
**MODEL:** White Truck
**INF:** One pair side emblems on hood

**#0059**

## WILLIES

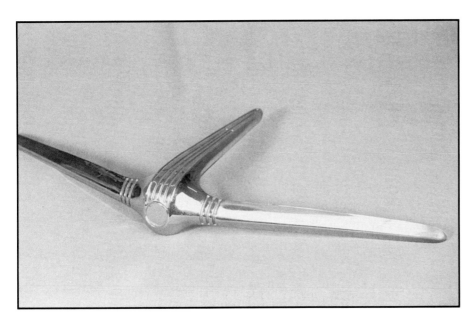

**YEAR:** 1950-1951
**MODEL:** Willies
**INF:** Jeep 9485
6777

**#0050**

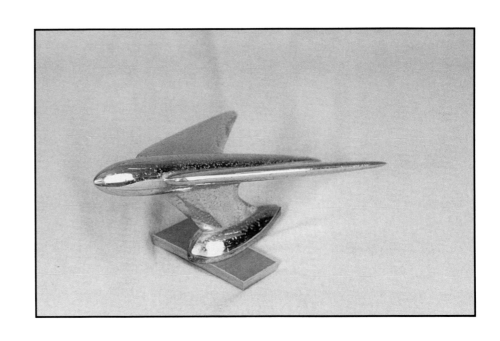

**YEAR:** 1953
**MODEL:** Willies
**INF:** 679823
Bird

**#0053**

U. S. Hood Ornaments and More . . .

# WHAT?

The units that are listed in this section are the ones that I have not identified. Many of these are original units and the balance will be reproduction units. If you are able to identify any of them please let me know. I know what some of the manufacturers are, but not the year for sure, thus I did not show them in the manufacturer section.

**YEAR:**
**MODEL:** What?
**INF:** Large blue dot; also red circle

**#0901**

**YEAR:**
**MODEL:** What?
**INF:** T1449443 Jet plane

**#0902**

U. S. Hood Ornaments and More . . .

# WHAT?

**YEAR:**
**MODEL:** What?
**INF:** Dog; not plated

#0903

**YEAR:**
**MODEL:** What?
**INF:** Crest
71902

#0904

**YEAR:**
**MODEL:** What?
**INF:** V; aluminum

#0905

U. S. Hood Ornaments and More . . .

# WHAT?

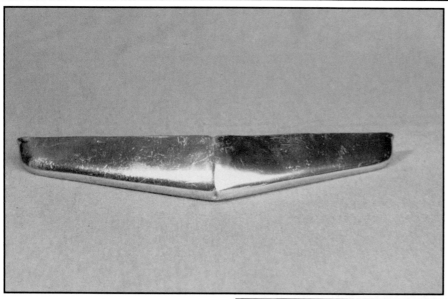

**YEAR:**
**MODEL:** What?
**INF:** Gold V

#0906

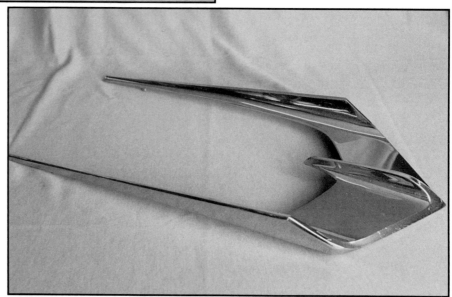

**YEAR:**
**MODEL:** What?
**INF:** 10-1/2" wide; 22" long

#0907

**YEAR:**
**MODEL:** What?
**INF:** Spring loaded 3" crown

#0908

*U. S. Hood Ornaments and More . . .*

# WHAT?

**YEAR:**
**MODEL:** What?
**INF:** BF7642528 9637
Overdrive script

**#0909**

**YEAR:**
**MODEL:** What?
**INF:** Plain chrome wing and tail; V mounting bracket

**#0910**

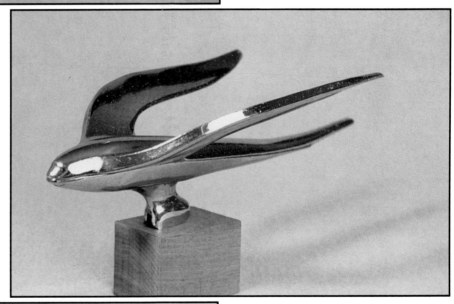

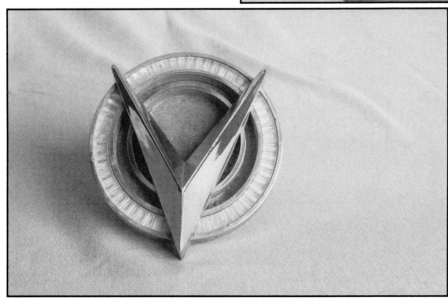

**YEAR:**
**MODEL:** What?
**INF:** V on circle
1187587 14082

**#0911**

U. S. Hood Ornaments and More . . .

# WHAT?

**YEAR:**
**MODEL:** What?
**INF:** Jet through ring

#0912

**YEAR:**
**MODEL:** What?
**INF:** Jet through ring

#0913

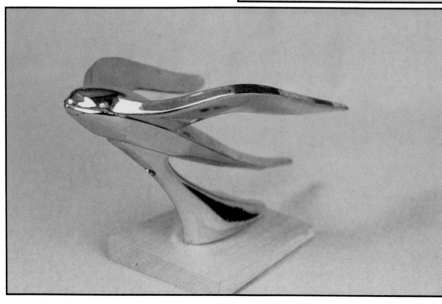

**YEAR:**
**MODEL:** What?
**INF:** Bird; top of wing & tail gold; chrome base & mount

#0914

U. S. Hood Ornaments and More . . .

# WHAT?

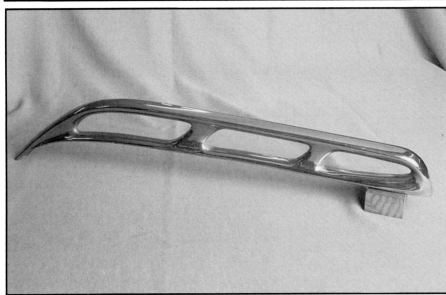

**YEAR:**
**MODEL:** What?
**INF:** Bridge design; 2" high; 20" long; 1961532

#0915

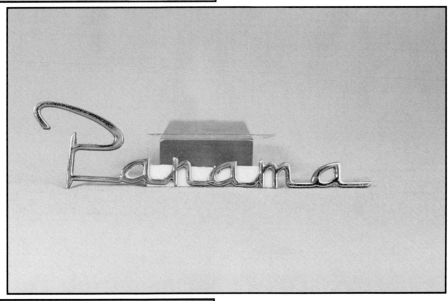

**YEAR:**
**MODEL:** What?
**INF:** Panama script

#0916

**YEAR:**
**MODEL:** What?
**INF:** Cast bronze truck; 8 1250-Y2

#0917

*U. S. Hood Ornaments and More . . .*

# WHAT?

**YEAR:**
**MODEL:** What?
**INF:** Bird in flight

#0918

**YEAR:**
**MODEL:** What?
**INF:** 1593434
Right fender;
Chrysler family

#0920

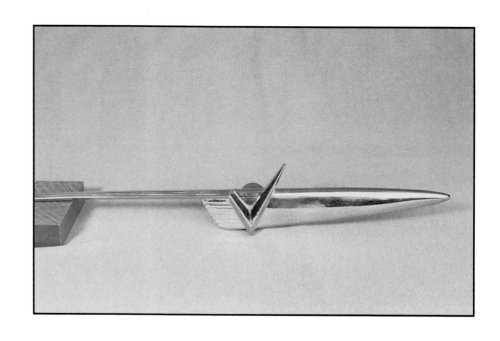

U. S. Hood Ornaments and More . . .

# WHAT?

**YEAR:**
**MODEL:** What?
**INF:** Flying horse with red wings

#0700

**YEAR:**
**MODEL:** What?
**INF:** Horse similar to White truck

#0701

**YEAR:**
**MODEL:** What?
**INF:** Swan with 6-ribbed tail

#0702

U. S. Hood Ornaments and More . . .

# WHAT?

**YEAR:**
**MODEL:** What?
**INF:** Hercules with lighted ball

**#0703**

**YEAR:**
**MODEL:** What?
**INF:** Flying lady

**#0704**

**YEAR:**
**MODEL:** What?
**INF:** Swan with 4-ribbed tail

**#0705**

## U. S. Hood Ornaments and More . . .

# WHAT?

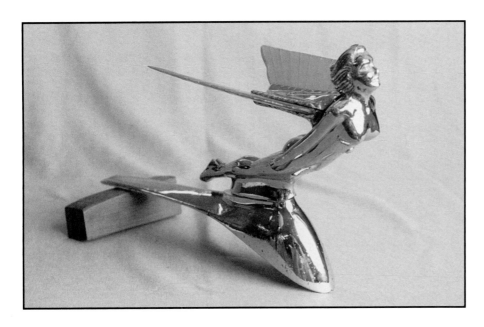

**YEAR:**
**MODEL:** What?
**INF:** Golden lady with red wings

#0706

**YEAR:**
**MODEL:** What?
**INF:** Ram

#0707

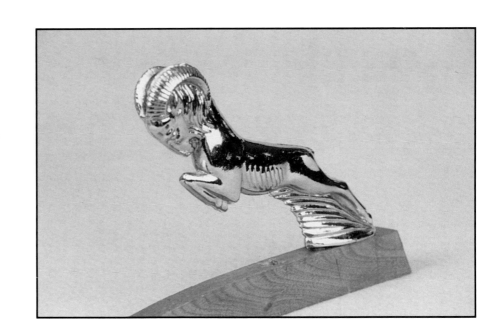